D1631178

COUNTRY TALK CONTINUED

COUNTRY TALK CONTINUED

J. H. B. Peel

ROBERT HALE · LONDON

© *J. H. B. Peel 1979*

First published in Great Britain 1979

ISBN 0 7091 7861 1

Robert Hale Limited
Clerkenwell House
Clerkenwell Green
London EC1R 0HT

Photoset by Photobooks (Bristol) Limited
and printed in Great Britain by
Lowe and Brydone Limited, Thetford, Norfolk

Contents

Other books by J. H. B. Peel include:

POETRY
Light and Shade

ESSAYS
Country Talk
More Country Talk
New Country Talk
Country Talk Again

TRAVEL
Portrait of the Thames
Portrait of the Severn
Portrait of Exmoor
Along the Pennine Way
Along the Roman Roads of Britain
Along the Green Roads of Britain
An Englishman's Home
Peel's England
All Over Britain

The love of nature is the first thing in the mind
of the true poet . . .

William Hazlitt

1

The New Familiar Faces

Despite his eighty years, the retired farmhand was active and alert. Even in bitter weather he would walk to 'The Wheatsheaf' for a pint of cider. Others came and went, died or were born, but he, like Tennyson's brook, seemed destined never to fail. Last week he died. I shall therefore miss his cheerful greeting on my walks. I shall feel tempted to sigh with Charles Lamb: "All, all are gone, the old familiar faces."

Time's tumbril does indeed appear to grow louder and more frequent as the years slip by; but that is an illusion, an inescapable quirk of human metabolism. Youth and prime do not suffer it. They are too busy to count the coffins. In any event, life itself shows no sign of giving up the ghost. On the contrary, the old familiar faces are perpetually being replaced by new ones, and if you look closely you will see that some of the latter bear a remarkable resemblance to some of the former. There are, of course, certain characters whose development we hesitate to predict: notably the so-called adults who wear shaggy beards, bell-bottom trousers, and a chip on each shoulder. Is it possible, we ask, that such persons ever will emerge from their cocoon of protracted and protesting adolescence? Other characters, however, do reveal the shape of selves to come—Joe, for example, the carpenter.

To some of us it seems only yesterday that Joe was a black-jerkined speed maniac with a fondness for revving his motorcycle at midnight. He arrived late for work and departed early. He mocked at matrimony, and regarded all people over the age of twenty-five as nine-tenths dead. Yet now he is a settled man with three children and the beginnings of a paunch. More than once he has been heard to say that the young apprentices take no pride in their work. Joe's grandfather may have passed a similar verdict on Joe's father, who certainly passed a similar verdict on Joe; and all three of them may have been partly justified. The point is, we feel reasonably sure of what Joe will be like in twenty years' time, at ease in the tap-room chair which his father now occupies. Youngsters will then call him "Old Joe", and to his grandchildren he will seem an eternal feature of the landscape, an oak that was planted long ago and will never be felled.

The effects of genes and environment are evident in Joe's fourteen-year-old boy, for father and son share several traits. They both like to sing the old hymns in church. They both thank God for a Queen who does not need to tout for votes on television. They both cheer when the local team wins, and when it loses they refrain from assaulting the referee. There are millions of Joes in Britain, and millions who will succeed him. That prediction must not, however, become too precise, because human nature does change with Time, in some ways for the better. Unlike his father, for example, Joe will never join the bell-ringers solely because the parson hinted that he ought to. Unlike his grandfather, Joe will never flinch when a car flashes past at fifteen miles an hour. Unlike his great-grandfather, Joe will never drink water in order that his wife may drink milk. Even so, it seems likely that Joe will remain true to the type whom Edmund Blunden admired:

> On the green they watched their sons
> Playing till too dark to see,
> As their fathers watched them once,
> As my father once watched me . . .

Since Joe was baptized and married at the village church, and has expressed a wish to be buried there, he shares a second resemblance to Blunden's countrymen:

> From this church they led their brides,
> From this church themselves were led
> Shoulder-high; on these waysides
> Sat to take their beer and bread.

One finds a comparable metamorphosis among the ladies. Ten years ago, for instance, Louisa was as pert a piece as ever came home at three o'clock in the morning and then expected to be served with breakfast in bed at noon. Her mascara was as ghastly as modernity could make it. Her clothes exactly resembled those which the Rag Trade had decided were most profitable to the Rag Trade. Louisa smirked and smoked and swore. She derided the qualities which men have admired since Eden—gentleness, modesty, domesticity and the broad-minded self-restraint which is best defined as chastity. Yet today, at the age of twenty-seven, that consumptive-looking scarecrow is the pink-cheeked wife of a gamekeeper, who, like their two children, marvels at Louisa's skill with the mop, the needle, the oven, the bandage. Instead of subsisting on serve-yourself tins, she has learned from her grandmother to cook such appetizing meals that her husband's pals—who are less capably married—often contrive to drop in at suppertime. The proof of Louisa's pudding is to be found in the words of one of those pals: "Tom, lad, I reckon you've married a winner. I only wish *my* old woman . . . never mind, it's too late now."

Places are, unfortunately, less resilient than people, less able to adapt themselves to change, for whereas a villager may assert his identity against a multitude of oppressors, a village will perish under a housing estate or a factory. Urban hours and industrialized relations soon unsettle the dawn-to-dusk rhythm of work on the farm. Under such a regime, men think more of their 'rights' than of their responsibilities. They leave the tractor in mid-field, eager to get home in time for television; even toward a generous master they feel neither loyalty nor affection. Yet there is a limit, surely, to the speed at which the British countryside and its inhabitants can be made other than they used to be. Evolution moves more slowly than Progress. Cars have not yet robbed us of the will to walk, nor propaganda of the power to think. Not in our time nor in our children's children's time shall Louisa and Joe become unrecognizable as the heirs of Blunden's countryfolk:

> These were men of pith and thew,
> Whom the city never called;
> Scarce could read or hold a quill,
> Built the barn, the forge, the mill.

A Cold and Frosty Morning

If you happen to be awake at dawn, your first glance through the window suggests that snow has fallen during the night; but when you wipe the misty pane, you see that the whiteness is frost. An hour later the brilliance sparkles under a cloudless sky. Three hours later it begins to melt under a mounting sun, at any rate in those places which the rays have reached. Elsewhere the grass is still covered by what might be mistaken for snow.

Climbing a meadow behind the house, you discover an even more dramatic contrast, because the frontier between green and white stretches in a straight line across the high moor, starting at about eight hundred feet and then rising to the summit at about eighteen hundred feet, where it creates a second frontier, this time between white and blue. Several images come to mind, if your mind works that way. You may fancy that the green and white frontier divides spring from winter, or you may decide that it divides youth from age, because the moor really does bear some resemblance to a young face crowned by white hair.

At noon the sun puts the final touches to a portrait of light and shade. In the light everything shines, and your vision becomes sharper, so that ivy encircling an oak looks like wet seaweed which has been rinsed by the tide. Clamped to a beech hedge, dead leaves resemble brown brocade. Meadows might be green pools whose waterside trees cast shadows over the surface, each tree bisecting itself, and each half being equally black. In some places even the twigs are imprinted on the grass. Ploughed last October, and then for some reason neglected, six furrows create their own contrasts. Four of them, in the shade of a hedge, are as hard as granite and as white as sugar; but the other two, basking in sunlight, are as brown as bread; and their ridges, though still hard, yield when kicked, unlike the frozen furrows, which merely bruise your toes. This is, in fact, the weather for arable farmers, the men who sow and reap a crop that requires capillary attraction (Latin *capillus*, a hair). The simplest way to illustrate capillary attraction is by dipping a piece of sugar into a cup of coffee and then observing the speed with which the brown liquid permeates the white lump. An analogy somewhat closer to husbandry is the speed with which the oil in a hurricane lamp travels up a piece of new wick. Every square foot of soil contains an uncountable number of hairs or tubes, all drawing moisture upward to the plant. However, the power of drawing up that moisture decreases with the size of the hair's internal diameter; the finer the soil, the more efficient the irrigation thereof. In short, something other than mere custom causes farmers and gardeners to plough and harrow and dig. Frost and rain help this human husbandry by alternately hardening and softening the soil, so crumbling it to a friable or pulverized tilth, able to draw moisture deeply during dry weather.

Up on the moor, meanwhile, conditions show little of the interplay between light and shade which varies the scenes in the combes and on the foothills. At nine hundred feet the land is covered with a film of frost that crackles when you walk through the heather, and hisses when you slip on a puddle. All liquid is frozen, unlike the water in the combes, which has thawed to swell the streams. No longer identifiable by their fringe of red grass, the bogs would cause some anxiety to a stranger, were it not that they, too, are as hard as ice. The shepherd, who usually gives them a wide berth, now uses them as a short cut.

At twelve hundred feet the wind is seldom still. This morning it rattles those dead leaves on the beech hedge, stirring the few wisps of fleece that sway like pendula from barbed wire and also from the lower branches of any stunted thorn that has managed to withstand the climate. While an arable farmer welcomes the frost, a hill farmer bends under a bale of fodder, knowing that not even the hardiest mountain sheep can exist on a diet of frozen heather. However, he does concede that frost is a lesser evil than the snow which may engulf his ewes and their unborn lambs.

At seventeen hundred feet the last lap of your journey reaches yet another contrast when you sight a patch of snow indented with pawmarks. Were the marks made by a rabbit, a sheep, a pony, a dog, a fox, or a stag? Was the animal walking, trotting, or galloping? The shepherd could answer those questions, and so could the huntsman. Thus, a walking sheep leaves an almost circular slot with a segment missing from the forward rim. A galloping sheep leaves a series of double indentations, rather like the two halves of an apple. The slots of a galloping red stag are unmistakable as pear-shaped indentations with a couple of small dots underneath. Animal droppings likewise vary with the species, offering another means of recognition. It is very cold on the summit or "out-over" as the country people say when referring to the high places of Exmoor. Here the snow lies several inches deep, dappled with pink and mauve sunlight. In some of the north-facing gulleys the snow may linger for several weeks after it has melted from lower ground and the south-facing summits (on Ben Nevis a few patches linger throughout most of the year). Screwing your eyes against the glare, you notice that the sun has passed its meridian and that several clouds will soon end its power to thaw. If the clouds disperse before nightfall, the frost may harden. But the sides of some of the combes are still sunny enough for their blue brooks to reflect Thomas Hardy's winterscape:

> And meadow rivulets overflow,
> And drops on gate-bars hang in a row,
> And rooks in families homeward go,
> And so do I.

On your own way home you re-enter the region of light and shade, where a copse beside the lane casts a shadow so black that you mistake it for a gap in the hedge. At the next bend, however, where the hedge casts its own shadow, a real gap admits the sun, which casts the reverse of a shadow, making it appear as though the dark lane has subsided, leaving a chasm or golden ha-ha.

When the Curtain Rises

Every year, during the first week of January, the great barn on Sir William's estate is inspected by two visitors. The taller of them, who wears a long greatcoat and a mane of white hair, can be identified as it were invisibly by his voice, which addresses every male as "Dear boy". The shorter visitor, who is of no recognizable sex but answers to the name of "Pinky", wears a mauve jacket and a toupee of yellow hair. He, too, can be identified by his voice, which addresses every male as "Darling" (and has a habit of adding *sotto voce* "Beast!").

The two visitors first met at Crewe railway station in 1930, when neither succeeded in borrowing five shillings from the other. Despite their long acquaintance, however, they show very little mutual esteem, for whereas the taller seems never to hear, the shorter seems never to heed, what his companion is saying. A more formal introduction might describe them as two elderly actors who in 1945 were engaged, at a fee of one guinea apiece, to enliven the local Victory Parade. Next year they were engaged to enliven Sir Richard's annual Orphans' Party, and thereafter they received an annual invitation to produce a New Year pantomime in the Tudor barn. Theoretically they come as guests of the Hall; in practice they lodge with the gardener.

On this latest revisitation the white-haired man gazed wistfully at the barn's raftered roof. "Time, as the Romans said, fugits. We are, my dear boy . . . without a shadow of doubt we are . . . well, not to beat about the bush . . . we are both sixty-nine years old. And by God I feel it."

"You look it, too," Pinky observed.

"I was about to say . . . are you listening? . . . to say that, in response to numerous requests, we shall again perform Dick Whittington." Here the ageing actor spun round on tiptoe. "Turn again, Whittington, Lord Mayor . . ."

"He wasn't."

"Wasn't what?"

"Lord Mayor. In those days they didn't have one. He was just Mayor."

"Pinky, dear boy, you were indeed educated at Upper Ammersmith Academy. Lights!" The last word was directed to the ceiling. "This time we shall place a lime in the loft."

"Is," Pinky asked, "the same old bitch playing Dick's mother?"

"The Countess will, as you say, repeat her triumph of yesteryears. And now, dear boy, to luncheon. In a word, to the kitchen."

"Bloody snobs," Pinky muttered.

"That may be. But say also, top-hole stew."

Pinky comes into his own off-stage, where he directs lighting, costumes and what he calls "dayportmon". The niceties of elocution, on the other hand, are divulged by the white-haired man, as when he says to Sir William's son, a cavalry officer: "My dear boy, you are indeed every inch a sole-dee-are. But . . . for this one evening . . . for this command performance . . . every yard of you must give the impression that you are unmistakably a purveyor of cat's meat. So, when you remind Dick Whittington of the days when you were lads together, may I earnestly exhort you *not* to say, 'Look here, old chap.' It would be incomparably more convincing if you could bring yourself to remark, 'Wotcher, Dickie-bird'."

To the gardener's six-year-old daughter the white-haired elocutionist whispers: "My child, let us rewrite your lines, even although Mr Pinky himself penned them. You are evidently puzzled by the word which you pronounce as 'fizzygonomy'. Let us . . . where's my pencil? . . . let us delete same and substitute the word 'face'. And, dearest child, could you . . . as a personal favour, which shall not go unrewarded . . . could you *not* pronounce the word as 'fice'? Now, let us try. Splendid! Bless you! Henceforth all men shall call you Sarah. The what? No, Maggie dear, not a Pop Group. Sarah was a Siddons."

Rheumatism, alas, now disbars Sir William from playing his role as the Cat; but Pinky has lately written a small part for her ladyship, which allows her to play the violin in Act One, to scatter toffees in Act Two, and in Act Three to lead the singing of *Auld Lang Syne*. Other regular members of the cast include a retired archdeacon, a very active major general, the postman, the sexton, Sir William's cook, and the huntsman's niece. Perhaps the most harassed member is the estate carpenter, who makes the scenery, works the lights, and combines the roles of Second Alderman and Cat's understudy. He was deeply disappointed when his *tour de force*, a stage trapdoor, was abandoned in 1972, after it had inadvertently ejected Robin Hood in the act of donning his trousers. When the players assemble for their first rehearsal, they are greeted Shakespeareanly by the erstwhile Hamlet: "Ladies and gentlemen, in this production the knight . . . and here I quote from the Bard himself . . . the knight, ladies and gentlemen, shall use his foil and target; the lover shall not sigh gratis; the humorous man shall end his part in peace; the lady shall say her mind freely.''

Last year the reporter from the local newspaper drank too much of cook's elderberry wine, and spent the entire performance on the floor in the men's dressing-room. This year he has written his critique in advance of the event, having been allowed to read the script beforehand and thereby to observe the skill with which Pinky has incorporated a line from Shakespeare, another line from Shelley, and more than another from the 1960 scenario of *Babes in the Wood*.

Come rain, come snow, the great barn is sure to be packed with villagers and their friends from outlying cottages and farms. At the first pantomime, in 1947, the most expensive seats cost two shillings; the cheapest now cost twice that amount; but the takings still go to charity. The front row of the stalls is reserved for the under-sixes; the second row for the Lord Lieutenant, the Bishop, the Admiral, the Rector, the MFH and a panorama of portly ladies. Owing to the spread of education, the huntsman (who used to work the curtain) and the gamekeeper (who used to serve refreshments) are now stationed in the loft, ready to restrain any young person who tries to leaven the applause with stink-bombs and cat-calls. Meanwhile, the village in general and the Hall in particular look forward to yet another pantomime that will bring happy memories to some, new enchantment to others, and amusement to all.

The Wide and Open Spaces

Indoor life has impaired our affinity with the open air and the myriad forms of creation that live in it. The average industrial man shuns the cold, and is easily overcome by heat. He seldom sees the dawn. He scans the stars through a lamplit haze. He assesses the seasons in terms of fuel bills and holidays; and although he may like to read about it while sitting by the fire, he would not willingly share the situation which Thomas Bewick relished: "To be placed in the midst of a wood in the night, in whirlwinds of snow, while the tempest howled above my head, was sublimity itself . . ."

George Sturt, an Edwardian carpenter, diagnosed an Aestheticism that is basically Philistinism: "Bottled Sunshine, Fresh Air through a meter, forms so large a part of Art, as though a man were married to a picture of his wife, instead of to the wife herself." Not surprisingly, therefore, most Britons feel uneasy when they do venture alone into a wild region of their own country. Some people would, of course, deny that Britain contains any wild regions at all. Siberians, one feels, would regard the entire kingdom as an overcrowded hothouse. Men from the Andes would in every sense look down on Ben Nevis, our loftiest mountain. A Bedouin might protest that even in Caithness a tourist has scarcely mounted his camel before he meets a car. Yet such things are relative. On the Sussex Downs, for example, between Firle Beacon and East Blatchington, you will find as much solitude as a sociable Englishman desires. Further west, in Hampshire, you will agree that Progress has not yet destroyed all those parts of Salisbury Plain which led W. H. Hudson to exclaim: "It was a joy to me to find such a spot in England, so wild and lonely."

Southrons look with awe on their Downs, but Hampshire and Sussex do not daunt the countryfolk who live north of Nottingham, or west of Hereford. Have you ever crawled up Knock Hush, that boot-bruising ravine near Cross Fell, the peak of the Pennines, overlooking Lakeland? Have you ever plodded across The Chains in North Devon, where Exmoor stands tiptoe above the sea? No trees grow there; if they tried to, the wind would cut them down. Have you followed the lane from Moffat to Beattock, where the hills are as bald as marble, and the blizzards so fierce that two coachmen froze to death while trying to deliver the Royal Mail? Have you climbed the stony track from Cwmann to Maesllan in Cardiganshire, or the old drove-road eastward from Tregaron? There is indeed a legacy of wildness still untamed in Britain; witness the Salt Way through Northumberland, a solitary slog among mountainous majesty near the Scottish border: no place, that, in which to sprain an ankle, or miss the path at twilight. Those are the wide and open spaces which led Gerard Manley Hopkins to ask a question and to express a hope:

What would the world be, once bereft
Of wet and wilderness? Let them be left,
O let them be left, wilderness and wet;
Long live the weeds and the wilderness yet.

Further north, Scotland's Rannoch Moor may claim to be
the most menacing desert in Britain. Even on a bright summer
morning the rocks and swamps lose little of their apparent
hostility. I once walked there all day, alone, feeling that the
sight of a house (which I never did glimpse) would prove to be a
mirage, the mind's last self-deception before it succumbed to
infinite monotony. Or there is the lane from Helmsdale to
John o' Groats via Forsinard in Caithness; you do pass one or
two houses on that long day's march, but they merely deepen

the sense of solitude. Hardly less hospitable are the Westmorland fells between Shap and Haweswater on the fringe of the Lake District, or the wind-worn desolation between Hartside and Alston in Cumberland, or the Derbyshire peaks above Buxton, or the emptiness which Sir Walter Scott sighted from Barnard Castle in County Durham:

> Westward, Stanmore's shapeless swell,
> And Lunesdale wild, and Kelton-fell,
> And rock-begirdled Gilmanscar,
> And Arkingarth, lay dark afar . . .

North, then, and west stretch the widest of our open spaces: the zigzag track to Brown Willy on Bodmin Moor in Cornwall; the rocky Abbots Way near Redmire on Dartmoor in Devon; the gusty heights of Charterhouse-on-Mendip in Somerset; the miles of moorland between Balmoral and Tomintoul, the highest village in the Scottish Highlands; the No Through Road to Bulpot Farm on the fells above Barbon in Westmorland; Mary Webb's Marcher country near the Long Mynd in Shropshire; and Hardy's haunted Egdon ("A face," he called it, "on which Time makes but little impression"). West, then, and north; yet the south and the east are not without their own unbeaten tracks. The Peddars Way, a grass-covered Roman road, fares very much alone on its journey from Ixworth in Suffolk to Holme-next-the-Sea in Norfolk, and never more lonely than along the steep sector from Fring to the outskirts of Great Massingham, an escape route favoured by smugglers during the eighteenth century. Away in Holderness, that sea-stolen coastline north of Hull, some of the signposts point only to a farm or to a cottage, the sole survivors of a village that has gone the way of Lyonesse. On the Lincolnshire wolds in winter you may wonder whether the natives are aware that cars have been invented. In winter, too, even the suburbanized Chilterns recapture something of their ancient isolation, as at Coombe Hill overlooking Chequers Court in Buckinghamshire or at Swyncombe Down overlooking Ewelme in Oxfordshire. On wet days between November and March you may fancy that Epping Forest is still a long way from Leicester Square; and a comparable seclusion pervades the Celtic ridgeway from Berkshire to Wiltshire. Likewise there are several solitary places among the marshes near Colchester; while down in Kent, if you know where to look, you will experience something of the shiver that seized young Pip when, having wandered from Joe Gargery's forge, he encountered a great unexpectation "in the dark flat wilderness beyond the churchyard, intersected with dykes and mounds and gates . . ."

2

Men of the Soil

There is no single routine of which one may say: "This, and only this, is the true country life." For instance, few men have loved the land more deeply, or better understood its multifarious activities, than did Viscount Grey who, as Foreign Secretary in 1914, had no need to dig his own garden, milk his own herd, plough his own fields. It is possible that he never undertook any of those tasks; and if he did undertake them, it was solely for the pleasure they yielded as tests of stamina and skill. Yet Grey was undoubtedly what we mean by "a true countryman". He returned to the country whenever his duties allowed; in the country he spent the best moments of his life, not as a spectator but as a participant whose knowledge of birds has passed into literature. Siegfried Sassoon saw him as literally a part of the landscape:

> In lichen-coloured homespun clothes he seemed
> So merged with stem and branch and twinkling leaves . . .

Grey was, in short, a notable example of the countryman who does not need to soil his hands, unless in play; who uses sport, not manual labour, as a means of maintaining bodily health and mental agility; who, at the end of each day, bathes, changes his clothes, and, having dined, takes a glass of port while pronouncing on a scholarly topic. At the other end of the rural spectrum is the man whose working hours are spent almost entirely out of doors, performing manual tasks as a means of livelihood. Having finished work, he will certainly wash his hands, but he seldom changes his clothes, and never at all discusses the finer points of an erudite subject. Although machinery has decimated the number of those men, the breed still exists and can be seen at its best among the farming community.

Who, then, are the truer countrymen—the landowners, or the land-workers? Perhaps the distinction is unnecessary insofar as the aforesaid extremes may to some extent be merged. One remembers John Clare, the agricultural labourer, who found time to read poetry and ultimately to write it. One remembers Count Leo Tolstoy, who often worked with the emancipated serfs on his estate at Krasny Rog. Truly the author of the world's mightiest novel was himself a mighty man, able for hours at a stretch to wield a scythe. Such people possess a passable knowledge of the elements of husbandry. They recognize the common birds and flowers, and some of the uncommon. They walk their footpaths, they assess their neighbours, they study the impact of current affairs on their locality. In all this they are, no doubt, merely the equals of many other countryfolk, but their travels have acquainted them with people and places beyond the range of the average cottager, and their reading has revealed the evolution of the landscape and the life of its inhabitants.

Much nonsense has been written about the so-called dignity of toil, and most of it came from persons who, if they had been required to drive a plough team, would have collapsed after the fifth wavering furrow. Manual labour can be as monotonous as mental labour. Nevertheless, a farmhand does at least hear the birds and see the flowers and the animals. Robert Bloomfield, a ploughman-poet, knew what he was talking about when he cited the satisfaction which comes from a worthwhile task done well:

> With smiling brow the ploughman cleaves his way,
> Draws his fresh parallels, and, widening still,
> Treads slow the heavy dale, or climbs the hill . . .

Robert Bridges was another who knew what he was talking about when—from the uppermost end of the rural spectrum— he confessed:

country life I praise
And lead, because I find
The philosophic mind
Can take no middle ways . . .

No amount of sentimental nonsense can alter the fact that
human beings need to make contact with the soil. This is
proven by the multitudes who relax and at the same time in-
vigorate themselves by mowing their lawn and by spraying their
roses. It is proven by the malaise which may affect those who
live in skyscraping tenements, cut off from all save a visual
contact with the concrete courtyard far below. It is proven also
by the townsfolk who, having withdrawn from the rat race,
seek a simpler and more rewarding existence in rural com-
munes.

Many migrants from urban areas now live in the country or
in quasi-country. One thinks of the numerous retired people,
of the commuters who make long journeys to a city, and of their
fellow-migrants who serve them in shops and offices. Although
it would be absurd to deny that some of those settlers are true
lovers of Nature, it would be equally absurd to deny that they
lack the roots which bind a lifelong villager to the land. "The
child," said Wordsworth, "is father to the man." In other
words, a countryman must be born at a very early age, for the
longer he postpones his introduction to the fields, the shorter
his apprenticeship therein.

Time will diminish the differences between the native and
immigrant populations in the countryside. A century hence,
these words—if anyone should then read them—may sound
like echoes from a vanished era, so deep and widespread will be
the effects of machinery and communication. When shepherds
watch their flocks by radar, and when commercial travellers
commute across the Atlantic, our own generation will seem
archaic indeed. At present, however, the most rural of our
rustics are born and bred in the country, and spend their life
there, often in the same district, sometimes in the same parish,
perhaps in the same house.

A Winter's Tale

"All our house was quite snowed up . . . the kitchen was darker than the cider-cellar. Several windows fell right inwards, through the weight of snow. We were obliged to cook by candle-light; we were forced to read by candle-light; as for baking, we could not do it, because the oven was too chill . . . Of the sheep on the mountain, scarcely one in ten was saved. That great snow never ceased for a moment for three days and nights." Those words from the forty-second chapter of *Lorna Doone* describe the blizzard which swept Exmoor three centuries ago, yet they might have been describing the blizzard which swept Exmoor during the winter of 1978; not, indeed, the most prolonged blizzard, but certainly the fiercest within living memory.

The first snowflake fell at dusk, hissing as it grazed the hurricane lamp which nightly shines outside my door. The air being still, each flake fell like a slow stone. Viewed through the window, the ballet seemed gentle and benign, as if an infinite series of dancers were concluding their performance with a curtsey. Birds, one felt, had nothing to fear; sheep could safely graze; and pylons would continue to stride like seven-league boots carrying comfort through the cold.

At sunrise next day this house and a large part of Devon and Cornwall awoke to a new world. In biblical terms, the valleys were raised while the summits were levelled. Every tree was piebald, its windward side wholly white, its leeward side wholly black. In a conifer plantation the drooping branches resembled icy arrowheads pointing a route to heaven. The sky burned blue, but not warmly enough to achieve a thaw. Since the house stands near the brow of a one-in-three hill and at some distance from a lane, it would be cut off until a venturesome farmer arrived with his tractor. The lane itself was a fairyland of untrodden snow. Downward it delved, a white and motionless tide under an arcade of glistening branches, some of which had been snapped by a burden of snow six inches tall. Only the holly berries broke the black-and-white ensemble, like little wintry suns defying the snow's ubiquitous omnipotence. The brook in the combe flowed black, and sounded shrill above the muffled silence. At noon the milkwoman arrived, three hours late, not in her customary van but swaddled chin-high on a tractor. It was all very enjoyable, as pretty as a Dickensian Christmas card.

Suddenly, at teatime, the wind got up, prodding a bank of dark cloud from the east, as though to confirm Coleridge's Alpine weather forecast:

'Twas a deep moan that spoke the tempest near;
Or sighs which chasms of icy vales outbreathe . . .

Once more the hurricane lamp hissed when the snow slithered onto it. Once more the valleys were raised while the summits were levelled. But this time the birds did have something to fear; the sheep could *not* safely graze; and a broken cable had already ceased to carry comfort through the cold. So, the shepherds were out, rescuing ewes; the roadmen were out, gritting lanes; the dairymen were out, lugging churns; and several fools were out, patronizing pubs (some of the fools were out all night, shivering in their stranded vehicles).

Then the real attack began. For a day and a night the wind whipped the swirling flakes, and when the snow did cease, the wind went on whipping the drifts until the drive to this house was blocked by a white wall fourteen feet high. On some parts of the moor the drifts were thirty feet high, tipped with a static bow-wave that had been caught and embalmed in slow motion. Twice I plunged up to my waist; once, to my chest. It took me forty minutes to cover less than a mile. Thousands of homes were without water, electricity, radio, television. Some lacked even a working telephone. Supplies of every kind were running low. But those of us who had retained the outmoded ways were able to keep warm and nourished as we heaped logs on the fire, hacked ice from the well, and lit candles and oil lamps.

For several days we were isolated from the rest of the kingdom: no post, no paper, no milk, no food, no road, no rail, no nothing. All activity ceased, except the business of keeping alive. Many people could not venture more than a dozen yards from their door; those who could, battled uphill and down, offering and sometimes soliciting a cupful of milk, or a day's hard labour digging out sheep. Alone on its hill, and miles from a village, this house became a half-submerged igloo in a land of everlasting snow. On the windward side, only the upper part of the upper windows admitted light. Day after day nothing came nor went. Rescuers had to be rescued. Snow-ploughs blocked the lanes they were unblocking. Sometimes we heard a helicopter's life-or-death mission. Finally, on the fifth day, food was dropped at the nearest village.

Our attitude to the blizzard remained ambivalent. On the one hand we relished a seclusion deeper even than our normal freedom from traffic. We gave thanks for our weather-proof roof and our thick stone walls. We enjoyed hearing about ourselves on the radio and television. We positively beamed whenever our villages and little towns were mentioned—South Molton, West Buckland, Lynmouth, Brayford, Simonsbath. But on the other hand we found that the prolonged incarceration bore too great a resemblance to the infirmities of age. We found also that some of our so-called necessities were mere luxuries and that several of them were time-wasting rather than time-investing. Not a few families found that they could spend an evening in pleasant fireside talk, or in reading a book, or in meditation. Inevitably, the young and the hale suffered less than did the old and the ill.

Thousands of cattle and sheep perished in that memorable blizzard, as well as an incalculable number of birds and other creatures. On my own forays I sighted the legs of two dead sheep sticking through a drift, and with my walking-stick I buried three frozen birds, one of them a thrush. Havoc, then, and hardship; much anxiety, some financial loss, and a few human lives claimed by the snow. Yet the old people who lived in market towns, or within sight of a snowbound main road, suddenly remembered that England in their youth had likewise been quiet, and intimate, and not overpopulated by strangers in a hurry.

Rook's Nest

A man from a Ministry stopped me in the lane the other afternoon, asking the way to Rook's Nest. When I pointed to a patch of derelict ground on the far side of the lane, the man seemed surprised, and wanted to know the name of the people who lived there.

"Ichabod," I told him.

"Icha who?"

"The people," I explained, "have departed."

"When did they leave?"

"Sixty years ago."

"Sixty? There must be a mistake." He flipped his sheaf of papers. "According to the Department of . . . yes, here it is . . . according to my information the house . . ."

"There is no house."

"But there must be a house. It says here it's called Rook's Nest."

"It *is* called Rook's Nest. But there's no house."

"Remarkable," muttered the man, and then drove on.

Rook's Nest is indeed remarkable, not as a departmental mistake but as an example of what happens when a few acres are allowed to run wild. During my childhood the place was a smallholding in a combe about fifty yards from the lane, to which it was joined by a steep and stony track. Old people can remember the last occupants, a hard-working couple who subsisted contentedly on a few acres. Today those acres resemble a battleground where the flora struggle for existence. The stony track—once wide enough to admit a horse and cart—has become a narrow path, criss-crossed with briars and fallen branches. The space between the path and the lane is a wilderness of leaves and weeds, through which a few primroses vie for a place in the sun. The space between the path and the brook—once a fertile field—has been taken over by snowdrops and Lent lilies which in February protrude through a lattice of twigs, fungi, docks, nettles, and bracken. Uprooted by gales, a huge tree at the far end of the path lies like a Norman pillar, its topmost branches pointing toward the lane. In its fall the tree carried away a semi-circle of soil, from which the roots hang like the ligaments of an amputated limb. In those ligaments a primrose thrives. Everywhere the decay and desolation are as bleak as a Brueghel winterscape and as horrific as a Disney nightmare. Encrusted with ivy and moss, the dead trees lean against the living, so that a breeze causes a perpetual creaking, rather as though a ship were chaffing a quay. The ground is so tangled with briars that only a gumbooted intruder can safely move there; and even then he must stoop to force his way between snapped boughs and the skeins of trailing ivy.

The ruined cottage creates a Gothic folly. There is no roof, no door, no window, and only such walls as suggest the general ground-plan. A zinc saucepan hides among the nettles, with traces of blue and white still visible under the rust. A blackened aperture at the base of one wall leads a stranger to suppose that it was the hearth at which the occupants cooked their food, warmed their hands, and heated their bath water. Since one section of the house stands within a few feet of the stream, it may have contained the kitchen. The nearest shop was and still is more than three miles away, up and down a one-in-three hill which in rough weather receives the full force of an Exmoor gale roaring from the sea.

A small disused quarry lies further down the lane, and it seems probable that Rook's Nest was built with stones from it. The lane being very steep, one marvels at the horses and men who hauled such heavy loads up the incline and down the track. What keen-eyed patience went to the making of that cottage; what picking and choosing to find the next piece in the jig-saw. By removing the ivy and then lifting the uppermost stones, you can perceive the skill with which they were selected and laid (a novice will spend as much time in choosing as in laying the stones; but a veteran will tell at a glance the best piece for the appropriate place).

Botanists would find much to interest them at Rook's Nest. Over the years I have watched the snowdrops and the Lent lilies spreading their white and yellow carpet, as though to bridge the gulf between January and March. Lately a sprinkle of bluebells has appeared, and they, too, will spread, forming a Maytime lake. In other places the perennial debris is so dense that only a spade could easily uncover the soil. You find first the newest fall of twigs; under that, the leaves of innumerable autumns; under that, a second layer of twigs, mouldy as mud; under that, yet more leaves, limp as sodden blotting-paper; and finally the soil itself, black and damp.

On winter nights, if you stand in the lane, you may hear a rabbit or perhaps a fox crackling among the undergrowth. Once—but only once—I heard a red stag sloshing through the stream. After heavy rain, the stream is audible; but in high summer you must stoop over it in order to hear the trickle. Very few birds build a nest there. No doubt they are deterred by the dead trees and prickly scrub. Few people ever see this ruin, though the fallen boughs and a portion of the walls are just visible from the lane. Yet the ruins must at some time have been visited, because every bit of timber has been taken from the cottage. Only a few Bridgwater tiles remain, like fragments of a flower-pot projecting above the nettles.

As for the man from a Ministry, I still wonder what led him thither. Was it Rates? Income Tax? Dog Licence? Insurance contributions? Or did the last occupants fail to register their own decease? We shall never know, for the mouldering stones tell only of Thomas Hardy's dereliction:

> we do not care
> Who loved, wept, or died there,
> Knew joy, or despair.

Looking Forward

A countryman's calendar is more vivid than a townsman's. Admittedly its rubrics do not always fall on a predestined day, yet they seldom fail to achieve a flexible punctuality. There is, for instance, the first snowdrop, followed by the crocus and the daffodil. There is the first full-throated thrush, the first lamb, the first cuckoo, the first bluebell. Likewise a countryman looks for the corn, the bud, the blossom. He marks also the coming of the swallow and the departure of the fieldfare; the first gale, the first frost, the first snow.

Year after year the commonplaces recur, and year after year a countryman is surprised by them. Though he may tread the same old mill, and sometimes feel as weary as Samson in Gaza, still he finds that each rung rises like a new day, identical with its myriad predecessors, yet utterly unique. All such rubrics look to the sun, which our primitive forebears hailed as the *fons et origo* of life itself. Despite their ignorance of Earth's axis and orbit, those ancient sun-worshippers were not wholly deluded, because springtime is the season when Earth reaches a given point on its circumnavigation of the sun. If, therefore, any single rubric does take precedence over the others, it must surely be the moment when we say: "The days are drawing out at last." Optimists, no doubt, will detect a difference on New Year's Eve, but not until February does the difference become something more than a relatively few minutes; and even then the number of minutes will vary from county to county, being greatest in the west of England and in the north of Scotland.

It is a curious experience, to look for spring amid the depths of winter; yet we do look, especially while walking in daylight at an hour which, less than a month ago, was steeped in moonlight. As the dusk settles down, so the colours fade. Hilltop woods resemble slabs of rich Christmas pudding, not quite black nor yet completely brown. Withered beech-leaves gleam like copper coins. Streams seem to be made of steel, and on them floats Hesperus, recalling the words of the Magi: "We have seen his star in the east . . ." So, a countryman says again: "This time last month it was pitch dark." Others are saying it too, albeit obliquely and in a different tone of voice. As the ploughman arrives home for supper, he remarks: "Dost know, I got back wi'out sidelights this evening." As the publican stirs the tap-room fire, he remarks: "I'm thinking it'll be a great economy no' to hae a fire so airly." As the gardener leans on his spade, he remarks: "Another five minutes of daylight, look you, and I'll have all these old leaves swept up I shouldn't wonder." As the gamekeeper unloads his gun, he remarks: "Sounds loike thart blackbird 'as put 'is clock on already. 'Ee were fair singing 'is 'ead orf." As the church bell strikes six, innumerable small voices remark: "Bedtime? But it's still light."

February is in many ways a teasing month. Its predecessor was wholly winter; its successor will be partly spring; but at Candlemas a countryman tends to do the splits by trying to stand with a foot in each camp. His senses tell him that February is winter and nothing but winter, for the leafless boughs and the lack-lustre herbage confirm Leigh Hunt's belief that spring's livery is green. "This," he said, "is the most apt and perfect mark of the season—the issuing forth of the Spring." But February grants no such issue. On the contrary, hay-wisps in meadows prove that the grass alone cannot sustain the livestock. Wayside verges are shorn, and a premature primrose merely emphasizes their wintry appearance. Many fields lie fallow and will remain so until a spring sowing. At a distant cottage—as in Edward Thomas's landscape— someone keeps the home fire burning:

> And, through the silence, from his shed
> The sound of sawing rounded all
> That silence said.

Besides, is not Candlemas—the Christian conversion of the Roman Lupercalia—is it not "a light to lighten the Gentiles"? Are not the candles necessary lights at Evensong? Do not the lights suggest an absence of light? And is not that absence a hallmark of winter? But the issue needs no oratorical questions, for the ewes in hill country have not yet lambed, and last week the ponds were frozen, and next week the lanes may be snowbound. Standing therefore on a windswept ridge, the countryman removes his leg from spring, and sets it where it belongs, in mud that may tomorrow become ice, on grass that will not revive until March, in twilight that has already sent the birds to roost.

And yet, and yet . . . is spring solely in the mind of the beholder? Are his intimations no more than wishes? He listens, and from far away, though all the other birds are dumb, one last thrush sings a final *Nachtmusik*. And after that—sheer coincidence, of course—after that a lamb in the combe utters its first beseeching sound. Tentatively the countryman once more stretches a leg toward April and May, knowing that his toecap has uncovered a snowdrop in flower and a Lent lily about to flower. Gradually the wind drops, as it often does at nightfall, and its going brings a kind of warmth. By the last of the lengthening light the watcher sees a beech bud, no longer a scar on a bract but already a recognizable embryo. Being keen-eyed, he detects a violet beside the lane. Being nimble-fingered, he lifts the fragile stem, and touches the tip of its folded flower. Then, with a glance at the sky, he makes for home, conscious that winter still reigns, yet confident that spring must be its heir:

> The pond will freeze, the dawn will scatter snow,
> The wind will comb the mountain with a rake;
> And yet tonight at last I surely know
> That spring remembers, and is half-awake.

The Lowland Highlands

On the main road between Carlisle and Glasgow, not far from Abington, a signpost points leftward to Leadhills and Wanlockhead, the two highest villages in Scotland, each outtopping Braemar, Tomintoul, and every other Highland settlement. Although the main road traverses a wild region, the noise and fumes from incessant traffic impair a full enjoyment of the scenery; but on the lane to Leadhills you very soon reach a Wordsworthian realm

Where earth is quiet and her face unchanged
Save by the simplest task of human hand
Or season's difference.

The lane twists and climbs among treeless hills speckled with sheep. Streams splash into the valleys, glinting like skeins of blue-and-white silk. Curlews call, circling in search of an answer. A derelict railway deepens the solitude. After about six miles you enter Leadhills, an aptly-named village, whose lead-mines were worked by the Romans and thereafter by the native Scots who littered the land with slag heaps.

Set on a windswept ridge, Leadhills consists chiefly of single-storey cottages that were built for the miners two centuries ago. Most of the cottages flank the narrow street; some are scattered below the ridge; all look snug and spruce. When the mining industry declined, the population of Leadhills fell to a few hundreds, yet in 1796 Thomas Pennant found "fifteen hundred souls supported by the mines". Lead poisoning, he added, caused "palsies and sometimes madness, terminating in death in about ten days". Despite the disease, John Taylor found the air bracing. He came to Leadhills when he was one hundred years old, and promptly sought work in the mines. After several decades of hard labour he died at Leadhills in 1770, more than 130 years old. But the best-known villager was Allan Ramsay, a minor poet, son of the local mine manager. Orphaned at the age of fourteen, Ramsay entered the wig-making trade at Edinburgh. In 1719 he opened a lending library, charging one penny per night per volume. In 1741, remembering his own childhood, he founded a Miners' Library Institute at Leadhills. The small building still survives, facing the Post Office. Like one or two other poets, Ramsay consorted with Venus and Bacchus, and then, like Adam, blamed Eve for his downfall:

Upbraid me not, capricious fair,
With drinking to excess;
I should not want to drown despair
Were your indifference less.

Although the Kirk never fulfilled its sixteenth-century dream of free and universal education, the average Scottish peasant was less uncouth than his fellows in England and

Wales. When an American tourist, Elihu Burritt, walked from London to John o' Groats in 1863, he observed: "You will seldom find a cottage in Scotland, however poor and small, without a shelf of books in it." Ramsay's bequests therefore, were in keeping with an attitude which made possible the achievements of Robert Burns, Thomas Carlyle, John Buchan, and many a son of the Manse.

Leadhills lies in Lanarkshire, scarcely two miles from Wanlockhead in Dumfriesshire. For many years each village claimed to be higher than the other, but the Ordnance Survey settled the matter by announcing that Wanlockhead stands 1,380 feet above the sea and therefore thirty feet above Leadhills. Unlike Leadhills, Wanlockhead is an untidy place, haunted by the ghosts of its miners. The houses trickle from the top to the bottom of several knolls, some of which appear to be slag heaps. The summits are bleak and bare; the lower slopes are pockmarked by centuries of digging. Here, too, Allan Ramsay founded a Miners' Institute. There is also a small museum with relics of the mines.

Thomas Pennant found little to admire in these parts. "Nothing," he declared, "can equal the barren and gloomy appearance of the country round: neither tree nor shrub, nor verdure, nor picturesque rock, appear to amuse the eye: the spectator must plunge into the bowels of the mountain for entertainment." Modern spectators, on the other hand, relish a bleak prospect, especially when they view it from a warm car. At Wanlockhead, however, the finest vistas can be seen only by travellers who walk the neighbouring heights. Northward in clear weather you sight Ben Lomond; southward, Skiddaw and Helvellyn; westward, Arran, Jura, and Ailsa Craig. In the neighbouring Lowther Hills gold was found; they say that some of it went to make the crown for King James V of Scotland.

Leadhills and Wanlockhead are among the dwindling number of places whose inhabitants follow the Celtic custom of living in *trevs* or small and separate communities. Until the coming of telephones and radio all such communities were the hub of their own universe. London was merely a name in outer space; its wars and woes and scandals hardly touched these highlands in the Lowlands. Even at their zenith the mines never spread far beyond Leadhills. The surrounding moors are still a vast sheep-walk, grazed by Cheviots, patrolled by shepherds. If you wish to discover how the eighteenth-century farmfolk lived and worked and played, you should consult Ramsay's pastoral idyll, *The Gentle Shepherd*, which serves as an antidote against George Crabbe and all other so-called 'realists' who are obsessed by whatever is harsh and dispiriting. Robert Burns paid a tribute to Allan Ramsay by asking and then answering a question: is there a Scottish poet who still writes about shepherds and the simple life?

> Yes! there is ane—a Scottish callan!
> There's ane; come forrit, honest Allan!
> Thou need na jouk behint thee hallan,
> A chiel sae clever . . .

3

March Winds

A shower of rain never kept any hale countryman indoors. To him a patter on the pane is as natural as the wind on the heath. But what happens when the weather fulfils Shakespeare's gloomy forecast: "The rain it raineth every day"? The rain hereabouts began at six o'clock last night, and was still falling at breakfast-time this morning, with never a break in the clouds. At noon the steady downpour became an erratic deluge, swept off-course by a north-westerly gale. Garden paths were puddled with wind-whipped lagoons, and the postman was forced to run the gauntlet of overhanging branches. Grass-blades—being unable to run—flinched whenever a cascade struck them. The last of the snowdrops mimed a tired metronome, each flower nodding half-wittedly. At lunchtime the BBC announced stale news: "In parts of the south-west the rain may be heavy and prolonged." At two o'clock it was evident that three o'clock would be lighting-up time. So, you rewrote Shakespeare, giving him an even gloomier gloss: "The rain it raineth every day; and also, my masters, it raineth throughout the day."

By mid-afternoon the murk becomes oppressive, especially to people whose livelihood is earned at home. The part-written page, or an unfinished canvas, seems irrelevant: "What's Hecuba to him, or he to Hecuba?" Instead of being a consolation, the log fire is a reward that has yet to be won; and until you have won it, the warmth remains valetudinarian, an invalid's cosseting, like calves' foot jelly and big black grapes.

When a voice from upstairs says: "Don't keep wandering all over the house. You know very well the carpets have just been shampooed"—when that does happen, then the following events are likely to occur: first, you tug yourself into gumboots, then you wriggle into an oilskin, then you clamp down an old cap, reach for a stick, whistle the dog, and—"For heaven's sake! Have you opened the front door?"

If, like myself, you live at the end of a long and tree-lined track, your walk to the nearest lane sends a tattoo of raindrops down your neck. Glancing up at the source, you step straight into the deepest lagoon, so that the muddy water splashes over and thence into your gumboots. Having reached the lane, you receive a gushing welcome from torrents that send twigs and leaves surf-bathing over your toes. One of the twigs floats as upright as a miniature caber.

At the first field-gate, where the grass has vanished in ankle-deep mire, an old Shire horse seems to be weeping, each tear a raindrop that wrinkles the brown Sargasso. Oaks sway slowly, like battleships in a seaway. Daffodils hang their penitential heads. The wind stings your cheeks, and sends the dog's ears aloft. At the next gate, habit causes you to halt in order to admire the vista, but you see only some sheep, fifty yards away, blurred by the rain. At seventy yards they merge with the mist. Suddenly the log fire seems less valetudinarian. Nevertheless, you plod across the field, no longer wincing when your footsteps splash your nose. Stumbling over a molehill, you reflect that yesterday you were gardening in sunshine, that tomorrow you may be doing the same again, and that in two months' time you may find yourself confounded by Browning's warning: "Though winter be over by rights, 'tis May perhaps ere the snow shall have withered . . ."

At the very moment when you begin to feel heroic after ten minutes' exposure to the elements, you come face-to-face with a man who has been out of doors since daybreak. He huddles under a hedge, with a sack over his head, sipping tea beside a brushwood tidemark that shows the extent of his labours.

"Blowing a bit," he remarks. "Fair drop o' rain, too."

"Yes," you agree. "March is a vile month."

"Just what we needed, eh?"

"But . . ."

"Do the grass a world o' good."

"Maybe, but . . ."

"I always did say, the weather turns up trumps in the end, though the end sometimes seems a long way off. Care for a swig o' tea?" He rummages in his wartime haversack. "I've got a spare mug somewhere. Ah, and the wife slipped-in an extra slice o' plum cake. Sit 'ee down. Make yourself at 'ome. Old Jeff Manning won't mind."

The hedge, you discover, really does create a windbreak; the sack diverts much of the deluge; the tea is as tasty as the cake. When you say so, the hedger looks pleased. "Her took first prize at the North Devon Show last year. In fact, the judges was like Oliver What's-'is-name 'cause they walked across and said, 'Missus, can us 'ave another slice?' "

The rain is still lashing when you arrive home. Smoke helter-skelters from the chimney, and a curtained window flickers red. Wondering why the rain is suddenly falling upwards, you notice that the dog has just shaken himself.

While disrobing in the porch, you hear the voice again: "The kettle's on. Tea won't be a minute."

"Actually," you confess, "I've had tea."

"Had it?"

"In Manning's Meadow. I met someone."

"Met someone? And then had tea in Manning's Meadow? In *this* weather?" Pause. "Are you sure you're feeling all right?"

The Coloured Counties

"You certainly see from this Bredon Hill one of the very richest spots in England . . ." So said William Cobbett, with special reference to the Worcestershire pastures: "The number of cattle and sheep feeding on them is prodigious . . . The sheep are chiefly of the Leicester breed, the cattle of the Hereford, white face and dark red body, certainly the finest and most beautiful of all horned cattle." Half a century later, Housman's Shropshire Lad and Lass climbed Bredon Hill in order to

>   see the coloured counties,
>   And hear the larks so high
>   About us in the sky.

John Masefield, a Herefordshire man, gave a more down-to-earth account of the prospect:

>   The apple trees in the orchard, the cattle from the byre,
>   And all the land from Ludlow Town to Bredon Church's spire.

Michael Drayton, a Warwickshireman, found Bredon's rounded summit more attractive than the Malverns' jagged silhouette:

>   And when great Malvern looks most terrible and grim,
>   Bredon with a pleased brow continually doth smile.

The name *Bredon* is a tautological amalgam of the Celtic *bre* and the Saxon *dun*, each meaning *hill*. In South Africa this Bredon Hill would be described as a *kop*, but British geologists call it a butte or conical eminence, topped by a stratum of hard rock. Bredon during the Dark Ages was called *Bruiden in Huic*, that is, the hill in the territory of the *Hwicce*, a tribe occupying parts of Worcestershire, Gloucestershire, and Warwickshire (where Whichford was *Hwiccaford*, 'the ford of the *Hwicce*').

Bredon Hill carries an eighteenth-century folly, Bell Castle, which stands a thousand feet above the sea, overlooking the Midlands and the Marches. Some climbers claim to have sighted fourteen counties from the Castle; some climbers, only eight counties; but the number scarcely matters, for springtime unfolds a pageant of primrose, daffodil, buttercup, daisy, bluebell, apple blossom, pear blossom, hawthorn blossom, and somewhere a strip of ploughland shining like a pink ribbon on a green garment. In Defoe's day the Worcestershire lanes were succulent as well as vivid. "We had," he wrote, "the pleasing sight of hedge-rows, being fill'd with apple trees and pear trees, and the fruit so common, that any passenger as they travel the road may gather and eat what they please . . ." Defoe's friend, the much-travelled Celia Fiennes, praised the Worcestershire panorama in her own brand of spelling and punctuation: "On the one side . . . lies Worcester Oxford Glocestershire etc . . . on the other side is Herrifordshire which appear like a County off Gardens and Orchards, the whole Country being very full of fruite trees etc, it looks like nothing else, the apple pear trees etc, are so thick even among their corn fields and hedgrows." In short, Bredon Hill offers a bird's-eye view of a truly English landscape. Northward lie the timbered villages of Elmley Castle, Eckington, and the two Combertons; southward the Cotswold stone glistens at Overbury, Conderton, Kemerton, and Grafton. The River Avon is there, and Eckington Bridge, scarcely changed since Quiller-Couch leaned on the parapet, hearing the pulse of peace:

> O pastoral heart of England, like a psalm
> Of green days telling with a quiet beat . . .

Since the Avon lacked a towing path, the barges sometimes hoisted sails. When going under a bridge, each barge was hauled by ropes that were passed over the parapet, carving a signature which Quiller-Couch identified as

> these eloquent grooves
> Worn in the sandstone parapet hour by hour
> By labouring bargemen where they shifted ropes.

Bredon village proves that not every picture-postcard tells a lie. There stands 'the Fox and Hounds', timbered and thatched, flanked by a drystone wall. Across the street, Masefield's "Bredon Church's spire" points a geometric finger *in excelsis*. Nearby, the fourteenth-century barn resembles a temple of Ceres, oak-raftered and stone-paved. Bredon, in fact, was part of a grange that belonged to the bishops of Worcester until the reign of Queen Elizabeth I. Having abolished the Church and the Prayer Book, Cromwell's republican saints imprisoned Bishop Prideaux at Bredon, allowing him the equivalent of six new pence per day for board and lodging. On such a diet, he complained, he would soon be compelled to eat his own books.

Edward Thomas equated a haymaking scene with the pastorals of "Clare and Cobbett, Morland and Crome". The scene from Bredon Hill is of a piece with the pastorals of Butterworth and Elgar, Drinkwater and Vaughan Williams. As the Midlands merge with the Marches, so a Saxon stolidity is leavened by a Celtic fey. Despite the nearness of Birmingham and other industrial zones, the people and places are rural.

Bredon Hill itself might be a hundred miles from anything louder than a tractor. One can therefore understand why John Drinkwater felt at ease in his Midland home:

> And, from this land of worship that I sing,
> I turn to sleep, content that from my sires
> I draw the blood of England's midmost shires.

Plotted and planted by Englishmen in their great days, the land hereabouts has not forsaken them in their decline. It is still a granary, a sheep-walk, a cattle ranch, an orchard. Blending duty and self-interest, the farmfolk rise with the sun, and in winter before the sun. As a merchant fingers the cloth, or a mechanic the machine, so a farmer knows when the soil is ripe for sowing, the hay for mowing, the corn for reaping. At all times of year, though never more vividly than in spring, Bredon

Hill affirms many good things. From the summit, gazing at the setting sun, a countryman answers "Yes" to Quiller-Couch's question:

> Lies it all peace beyond the western fold
> Where now the lingering shepherd sees the star
> Rise upon Malvern?

Birth of a Farmhouse

A north-country estate agent recently announced the sale of a property which he described as a fourteenth-century farm-house. If the agent meant that parts of the house were built six centuries ago, he was probably correct; but if he meant that they had been built *as* a farmhouse, he was probably incorrect, for mediæval England contained hardly any farmhouses as we now know them. A fourteenth-century yeoman lived in the town or village nearest his land, partly because he feared isolation and partly because the scattered allotments of feudal husbandry held no place for a nucleus of farmhouse and outbuildings. The word 'farmhouse', in fact, was not recorded until 1598. Most of our farmhouses are less than four centuries old, and many are less than two centuries old.

The Commander's house is an example of that evolution. It was built by a retired judge in 1573, whereafter it passed to a pirate who had plied his trade so briskly that he was able to extend the Long Gallery and to erect the spacious stables. In 1657 the house was acquired by Ezekiel Higgins, a Crom-wellian ploughman and keen amateur preacher, who, on being promoted to the rank of colonel in the rebel army, evicted the rightful owner, took possession of the place for himself and then named it Redemption Hall. Three years later, when King Charles II returned, the rebel fled, and the rightful owner resumed residence, albeit ruined by the fines that had been imposed on many royalists.

In 1663 Redemption Hall passed to a penniless younger son who, having rented some adjacent fields, set up as yeoman. In 1664 the stables became shippons, and in 1666 a pigsty was added. Thirty years later the entire village was bought by one of the Commander's ancestors, a nabob in the East India

Company; only Redemption Hall resisted the take-over, maturing like wine while the years of endeavour transformed it into a farm whose various inheritors could say, with Christina Rossetti:

> Woodpigeons cooed there, stockdoves nestled there;
> My trees were full of songs and flowers and fruit . . .

In 1730 the nabob's grandson married a Roman Catholic who persuaded him to join the Jacobites. During the '45 he escaped to France but could not evade a crippling fine; and although a brace of prize-taking admirals soon afterwards retrieved the family from its misfortunes, three successive male heirs died in action during World War I, and a large part of their resources was consumed by death duties.

In 1922 the estate was sold to a Lancashire mill-owner who had migrated south in search of an uncommercial status. During all this time Redemption Hall remained the property of Nonconformist yeomen, passing from father to son and from brother to brother until 1948, when the male line died out, causing the surviving spinster to put her heritage on the market, where it was bought by the Commander. Today, therefore, the old sailor owns a sixteenth-century residence, flanked by outbuildings which more or less fulfil his needs as a farmer of two hundred mixed acres. He sometimes reminds people that the only house he does own is the only house in the district which his forebears did *not* own. Feeling that the name 'Redemption Hall' was unctuous, he re-baptized the place 'Moat Farm' because a moat does encircle it. This defence was built in 1803 by an occupant who, fearing a French invasion, buried his money in the water (from which it was stolen by the shepherd's cousin, a descendant of Colonel E. Higgins). Though narrow, the moat offers a passage to the punt which is moored alongside the timber bridge, and enables the Commander's six-year-old grandson to lay the foundations of a naval career. The child is especially fond of shouting "Full astern!" and "I'm coming alongside." Having lately learned to swim, he still feels disappointed that the water is only three feet deep.

The hub of the house is the panelled Long Gallery, known to the family as The Cabin. Two-thirds of it serve as the

Commander's office-cum-snuggery; the rest, concealed by a curtain, contains his workshop and an array of gadgets and tools. As one might expect, The Cabin is an amphibious haven, decorated with a rainbow of rosettes for prize-winning heifers and cocker spaniels, as well as a photograph of the farmer as a midshipman, and a sketch of the cruiser in which he was wounded. Although the innumerable missives from government departments are classified with a precision that would please the Supply and Secretariat Branch of the Service, the Commander's private opinion of those time-wasting chits is expressed by one word, printed in red capitals on the filing cabinet: BUMF. Since the Commander's part-time crew are old seafarers—a naval rating and a Royal Marine—they sometimes refer to windows as "scuttles" and may steer the tractor "Hard to starboard!" The Commander himself will sometimes tell his two haymakers: "I'll join you on the Forenoon Watch."

Above the door to The Cabin hangs a map of the village, drawn in 1701, marking the manor house, rectory, smithy, inn, and every homestead except Redemption Hall, whose Dissenting independence the nabob preferred to ignore. This map proves that in 1701 several fields were still divided into feudal strips and that the present housing estate was then common grazing for manorial tenants. In a history of the parish, written by the rector in 1873, the Commander found a reference to his own home and its feud with the nabob: "The old farmhouse, known as Redemption Hall, has been in possession of the same family for more than two centuries. A path from the Hall to the Wesleyan Chapel was closed by the lord of the manor forty years ago."

Such, in brief, is the story of Moat Farm, the home of a judge, then of a pirate, then of a rebel, then of generations of yeomen, and now of a retired naval officer who farms his own fields, and hopes that his grandson will one day farm them despite Wedgwood Benn and other Leftward lurchers.

A Shepherd and His Dog

At certain times of year my two small fields are grazed by livestock belonging to a local farmer. This arrangement is mutually profitable because the farmer gets free grass while I get free manure and am moreover saved the cost of scything. Since every sheep is a potential Houdini, my non-paying guests are either cattle or a horse. The other day, however, one of the fields did contain some sheep, as well as a farmer who was training his young Border collie.

The rapport between a shepherd and his dog is as wonderful as the intelligence of the dog itself, a contrast indeed with a sheep's proverbial silliness. Yet the sheep know a thing or two, as was proven by the pair which, having been transported from Derbyshire to Kent, became so homesick that they walked back to Peakland, where in due course their horns were hung in the parish church. If, as some scientists assert, all creatures are merely biochemical machines, the machines may nevertheless marvel at their own reflexes. James Hogg, the Scottish shepherd-poet, declared that, without dogs, the mountains and moorlands "would not be worth sixpence. It would require more hands to manage the stock of sheep . . . than the profit of the whole stock would be capable of maintaining".

The two ancient breeds of sheepdogs are the Bearded Collie and the Old English Sheepdog, each having a shaggy coat and a rounded skull. First recorded in 1561, the word *collie* meant *black*. Shakespeare, for example, wrote of "the collied sky", and Sir Walter Scott referred darkly to "curs called collies" (but we cannot be sure that he was indicting the breed as we now know it). Some of the Border Collies have a black-and-white coat; others have a black-and-tan; a few, the merles, are black-and-grey, with blue eyes instead of the customary brown (some of the merles have one brown eye and one blue, which gives a false impression of blindness). When shepherds say that a dog possesses a keen eye, they mean a keen power of concentration, an important asset because dogs can mesmerize a flock simply by staring at it. Some, indeed, stare so hard that they mesmerize themselves, thereby wasting their master's time.

But, you may ask, why did the farmer choose to train his dog in my paddock rather than in one of his own meadows? There were two reasons why: first, the farmer and his dog and six sheep happened to be passing while I was mending the wire: second, six sheep in a small field are especially suitable for training a young dog, partly because the dog may chase the sheep and partly because the chase can be easily checked in a relatively confined space. If a dog does run amok on the hills, he may cause the sheep to plunge down a ravine, or entangle themselves in barbed wire.

Every sheepdog must learn to understand and obey five commands: "Heel", "Lie down", "Come on" (toward the sheep), "Come bye" (to the left), "Come away" (to the right). A well-trained dog will answer also to "Steady" and "Go back" (that is, in search of sheep hidden by a hill or some other feature). Most dogs have an instinct to drive sheep toward their master, but to drive them away from him is a skill demanding practice. Although the methods of training will vary from man to man and from place to place, all combine verbal with visual commands. In Wales last winter I saw a shepherd raise three fingers of his right hand, whereupon the dog retrieved three ewes. In Devon last summer I saw two collies co-operating like a hooker and a scrum-half, each fulfilling its own task, and neither attempting to usurp the other's.

Most shepherds carry a crook, and most crooks have a hazel shaft with a horn head. A crook's importance is symbolized by the crozier borne before bishops and abbots to signify their role as pastors of a flock. But the modern shepherd's crook is by no means an archaic totem; on the contrary, it is a necessary item of his equipment, as was shown by the farmer in my field, who, when a sheep did try to escape, extended his crook, caught the runaway by the neck, and brought her to a halt. It all seemed so simple, yet I had long ago learned that, when the shepherd is himself a novice, the sheep sometimes have the last laugh while they watch their would-be captor lying flat on his face in the mud.

The new metal crooks, which are cheap to buy and light to carry, find little favour among older men in deep country. I once spent an hour talking to a shepherd on the hills above

Hawick, and all that while he was sandpapering the horn of his new crook. "I'm thinking I'll add a dab o' varnish," he said. " 'Twill gie it a gloss and protect it agin the weather. Ye'll note, by the way, that the horn's no' white 'cause whiteness means immaturity, and immaturity means softness, and softness means an airly breakage. My auld crook belonged to my feyther. He made it himself, half a century ago, and it would still be alive if some half-wit hadna' crushed it wi' his tractor."

Shepherds tend to live long, no doubt because they walk much in the open air, or used to, until motors persuaded them to sit down (in Hampshire last month I saw a shepherd driving his flock while he sat at the wheel of a car whose smouldering clutch could be smelled one hundred yards away). The oldest working shepherd of my acquaintance is a septuagenarian among the Shropshire hills. When I last saw him, on an icy afternoon, he might have been John Clare's shepherd,

> in great coat wrapt
> And straw bands round his stockings lapt
> With plodding dog that sheltering steals
> To shun the wind behind his heels . . .

4

The First Real Day of Spring

If love and death are indeed the themes most favoured by poets, then it may be said that spring comes galloping home as an honourable third; but whereas the first two runners are seldom serene, the third is more often glad than sad. Poets themselves, however, feel ambivalent toward the spring. At one moment they praise it; at the next, they upbraid. Shakespeare welcomed the April flowers "that paint the meadows with delight". Nashe rejoiced because "the pretty birds do sing". Carew bade good riddance to a white Christmas and an icy Easter:

> Now that the winter's gone, the earth hath lost
> Her snow-white robes; and now no more the frost
> Candies the grass . . .

Nevertheless, some very harsh things have been said about spring. Andrew Young disliked its late arrival and early departure:

> So late begun, so early ended!
> Lest I should be offended
> Take warning, spring, and stay
> Or I might never turn to look your way.

The first day of spring is a debatable rubric. Some people define it as the day when the clocks are put forward; others as the day which fulfils their own concept of spring; and all are conditioned by the British climate, so that an Aberdeenshire fisherman remarks on the mildness of the air while a visitor from Cornwall complains of feeling cold. When spring does arrive, it travels northward at about one hundred miles a week, which is why the daffodils in Devon are dead before the daffodils in Durham have reached their prime. Spring, then, announces itself in March, comes to the fore in April, and withdraws in May. It is an ancient pageant, familiar yet forever fresh, like the re-reading of a great poem, or the reunion with an old friend. To some it is an affirmation that "all manner of things shall be well". Even a pessimist allows that the three months are vivid and fragrant and musical. As Landor observed: "Sad is the day, and worse must follow, when we hear the blackbird in the garden and do not throb with joy." It is as though life delights to see itself perpetuated, even as a man smiles on his grandchildren.

The arrival of a season may blur the fact that all seasons impinge on one another. For example, the blackberry skeins in April still bear a few rusty old leaves alongside the new ones, some of which are green, some gold, some the colour of ripe strawberries. So it is with the beech hedge, where autumn's withered foliage crackles against spring's greening buds; so also with the ferns whose tattered relics overlap the young fronds. A few Christmas berries still shine among the holly trees, and it certainly comes as a surprise to notice chrysanthemums peering above the soil, accompanied by Michaelmas daisies and a dahlia. During the second half of April the sun stealthily opens the buds while it shrivels the crocus, spills the blossom, and lures the lizard. Wherever you look, something is afoot, from the first fledgling to the last Lent lily, and from the last catkin to the first wallflower. Yet all this seemingly sudden upsurge is gradual and at times imperceptible because there are no moments at which a countryman may say: "This morning the grass began to rise." Any farmer will detect the growth of his herbage, but none can make a graph of its daily progress.

Although Nature disregards the calendar, she observes her own punctuality. The first swallow is seen year after year within a few days of the previous sighting. Birds mate despite the weather; come rain, come shine, they work a sixteen-hour day, feeding their voracious breed, defending their private

plot. Lambs frisk through the meadows, watched and sometimes warned by ewes whom motherhood has mellowed into
mutton. Young calves wobble on spindly legs while young deer
bask where the bee sups, hidden among yellow gorse. Down by
the sea, blue-jerseyed veterans slap tar on upturned dinghies,
hailed by a yachtsman homeward-bound from the year's first
voyage across the bay. Deck chairs appear. Hoes clink in
cottage gardens. The Gents' Outfitter replaces his winter
woollies with a display of linen jackets. Most emphatic of all is
the cuckoo, that repetitively vocal calendar. The land waits, as
Sidney Keyes watched it wait, certain of fulfilment:

> Wise be the woods, and every pale-throated
> Primrose at peace . . .

Why, then, did Sir William Watson liken early spring to a
fickle girl? It was because Worcestershire fruit-growers may be
ruined by an hour of midnight frost, because Leicestershire
graziers may find their grassland set back by a week of searing
wind, because Perthshire postmen may dig their way through
six feet of snow, and because a Boat Race crew may go down
like the fighting *Téméraire*. Yet the spring prevails, and the
corn ripens, and we do not starve to death. Despite gales and
snow and rain, our spirits rise and shine as though, like the
flowers, they, too, draw sustenance from the lengthening
daylight and the rising temperature.

Insofar as it succeeds winter, spring is new; insofar as it has
been doing so for some considerable time, spring is old. Old,
therefore, and new, spring eludes an original comment on
itself. "*Pereant isti*," growled the Latin playwright: "Damn the
fellows who've already said what I'd intended to say." Wiser
poets accept the inevitable, and do not wrack their brains for
unnecessary ingenuity. Siegfried Sassoon pitied the man who
will not speak unless he feels certain of sounding original:

> And then with nothing unforeseen to say
> And no belief or unbelief to bring
> Came, in its old unintellectual way,
> The first real day of spring.

The April Muirburn

Akroyd, the gamekeeper, is in some ways behind the times and in other ways abreast of them. Seen from a distance, he resembles an Edwardian, for his Norfolk jacket reaches almost to his knees, and his stalker's hat—which once belonged to the head keeper of the present squire's father—was discovered in a hatbox that had lain unnoticed in a loft above the stables.

Renovated by the village saddler half-a-century ago, Akroyd's gamebag still wears well and looks well. Despite these old-fashioned foibles, Akroyd is only twenty-nine years old and, so far from being set in his ways, has lately taken a fiancée. He made his choice while walking home *à deux* from a supper which the girl had prepared for himself and her widowed father. Although he speaks only when speech is unavoidable, Akroyd rose to the occasion by remarking: "Thy roast potatoes were champion. Happen they're near as good as my own mother's." After proceeding in silence for another half mile, he stated that a marriage was desirable. During the course of the next half-mile, the girl (a Yorkshire farm-lass) replied: "I mun think on't." Some days later, apropos of nothing in particular, she said to Akroyd: "I've been thinking. Happen thou's reet."

Gamekeeping demands a knowledge of stoats, foxes, heather, weather, weasels, climate, bogs, game laws, bird protection laws, and poachers. A gamekeeper must know also the merits and defects of a Doctor Deadfall, a Macpherson, and the Euston System. Although his territory may be smaller than a huntsman's, it requires an even closer acquaintance, for of what use is a keeper who spends time and money on snaring rabbit-holes without ascertaining whether they are occupied? Akroyd began his own pupillage by registering a black mark which he took to be a jackdaw. Drawing his gun at a venture— he was then twelve years old—he winged a raven, and so registered a second black mark because ravens are protected by law. He was alone at the time, but the Perthshire mountains carried the sound of his error to an under-keeper who promptly delivered a sermon on *Corvidae*, followed by a

warning to aspiring gamekeepers: "If ye've no' a mind to
commit premature professional suicide, just remember this
. . . be eupractic, mon, be eupractic." News of the incident
travelled faster than Akroyd, who, on arriving home and in-
quiring the meaning of "eupractic", was told by his mother:
"It's a bairn who doesna' break the law."

Akroyd's father had migrated from Swaledale, and was
tending Cheviots for a laird who accepted Akroyd junior as an
apprentice, first in the kitchen, then in the gardens, next as a
beater, and eventually as an under-keeper on the laird's grouse
moor in Yorkshire. Those Scottish years, together with six
months on an arable estate in Hampshire, ensured that Akroyd
became an all-rounder who had shot wild cats, stalked red deer,
and fed open-range pheasants four times a day, not forgetting
to give the chicks a morsel of hard-boiled egg.

Many townsfolk regard a gamekeeper as one who occasionally goes for a stroll, carrying a gun with which he occasionally
shoots pigeons and rabbits. But that is only part of his work,
for there would be no game to preserve unless he had reared it,
a long and often tedious task, a perpetual battle against disease
predators, climate. Even when young pheasants have been
moved to covert, they must still be fed twice a day and trained
to come when called. Only huntsmen and shepherds can vie
with a gamekeeper's knowledge of country life, its flora, fauna,
geology, husbandry, customs, crafts, and cottagers. At an hour
when most townsfolk are still asleep, a gamekeeper is up and
away on the moors, or through the woods, or across the
meadows.

Akroyd's constant companion is a lemon-and-white spaniel.
In public he treats the dog as he treats his gun, carefully yet
unemotively; but when there is nobody to see or to hear him,
he expresses his deeper feelings and would, if he could, speak as
eloquently as Siegfried Sassoon:

> What share we most—we two together?
> Smell, and awareness of the weather.
> What is it makes us more than dust?
> My trust in him; in me his trust.

At this time of year Akroyd is busily burning or swaling the
heather, a task which he calls "making a muirburn", an echo

from his Scottish boyhood. If heather is allowed to grow unchecked, it produces thick and woody twigs. A grouse moor is therefore burned in order to give the birds a diet of fresh herbage. The burning may prove difficult and at times impossible if rain and snow render the heather incombustible. Scottish law has controlled the making of muirburn since 1772, but no closed season was imposed on England and Wales until 1949, when swaling was banned between the end of March and the beginning of November, except by permission of the Ministry of Agriculture. Akroyd burns his heather in strips and against the wind, so that the airborne seeds will fall on blackened areas. He starts the fire by means of an oil lamp with a long handle and a long spout. This he calls "the Mac" because it was first sold by Macpherson of Inverness. If heather in March is still sodden, the keeper may—like Akroyd—seek permission to burn it during April, or at some time thereafter. If permission is granted, the fire will probably destroy the heather-blighting beetles which, since they hibernate under the soil, can survive an early burning. Akroyd himself believes that the beetles thrive on damp patches, so he arranges for the soil to be drained by a contractor. Unlike some of the Dartmoor commoners, he burns his heather only when it shows signs of age. Excessive burning does more harm than good. Akroyd, indeed, says that it does no good at all: "Some folks are like a pack of kids. They just want to see a bonfire."

Although gamekeepers no longer need to wage war against starving poachers, they do need to beware of professional criminals in fast cars. If a local thief is caught, he may exhibit the pertness of Richard Jefferies' poacher, who, when the magistrate warned him that many people had heard about him, replied: "Yes, my lord; but people don't never hear nothing about *you*."

Season of Colour and Scent

Spring and summer are the most fragrant seasons and probably the most colourful, though some gardeners may feel that nothing excels the splendour of roses and antirrhinums mingling with dahlias, chrysanthemums, and the first autumnal tints. Actually, there is no season nor even a single day when the British countryside lacks a flower in bloom. While many people suppose that flowers are mere ornaments, other people make an even greater mistake by supposing that the ornaments were devised solely for the delectation of mankind. It would be more to the point to remark that flowers sustain mankind by

absorbing noxious gases and by producing medicinal salves, such as morphia (a pain-killer so effective that science has failed to concoct a comparable synthetic substitute) and digitalis, the leaves of foxgloves, *Digitalis purpurea L* (a palliative for certain cardiac diseases). From the autumn crocus comes the best anodyne against gout, from liquorice comes a defence against gastric ulcers, from the willow tree comes a tranquillizer, and from the periwinkle comes vinblastine for the treatment of cancer.

In mediæval Britain every monastery cultivated a herb garden for both medical and culinary purposes. When St Bartholomew's Hospital was founded by Rahere, the King's jester, its physicians treated leprosy with burdock, goosegrass, and garlic, which are still used in the manufacture of drugs. When Sir William Harvey discovered that our blood circulates throughout the body, he wrote his treatise in Latin; but an earlier scientist, William Turner, Dean of Wells, wrote *A New Herball* in English because, he said, "many a good man was put in jeopardy of his life" by physicians who could not translate a Latin prescription. At Chelsea in 1673 the Society of Apothecaries opened Britain's first public Physick Garden, thereby adding a utilitarian gloss to Francis Bacon's maxim: "A garden is the purest of human pleasures."

Many flowers are so beautiful that their role as a necessity has been overshadowed by their role as a luxury or (in Dr Conan Doyle's phrase) "an embellishment of life". Flowers, in fact, vie with birds as the poets' favourite feature of a rural scene. All the great English poets have written memorably of flowers. Wordsworth asked for a flower to be carved on his gravestone. John Clare certainly made no apologies for the profusion of his own posy:

> My wild field catalogue of flowers
> Grows in my rhyme as thick as showers,
> Tedious and long as they may be
> To some, they never weary me.

Tennyson regarded flowers as a key to the mystery of life:

> if I could understand
> What you are, root and all, and all in all,
> I should know what God and man is.

The most comprehensive of our floral poems was written by Robert Bridges, himself a physician, who named eighty-three plants in nineteen stanzas:

> Blue-eyed Veronica
> And grey-faced Scabious
> And downy Silverweed
> And striped Convolvulus.

If cowslips really are the first flowers of spring (*Primula veris L*), what are the first flowers of winter? Botanists tend to give two answers. At first they will say: "There's no such thing." Then, as an unacademic afterthought, they may add: "Daisies". First or last, the floral cycle spans the seasons, and in January—when snowdrops outshine their namesakes—a countryman begins to think of spring. Then come the Lent lily and its stately relative the cultivated daffodil. Crocuses, too, are in bloom, truly gemlike and a prey to thieving bullfinches. Primroses follow next, sometimes flowering in winter, though they wait until April before shining *en masse* like pools of pale sunlight. When the primroses have faded, the woods and banks are paved with bluebells, the most beautiful of all our wayside flowers. Yet none of these is heavily scented. The year's first strong perfume comes with the wallflower.

Despite television and weekend motoring, most villagers still find time to maintain a tradition which William Cobbett admired: "You see," he wrote, "in every part of England . . . that which is an honour to England, and distinguishes it from the rest of the world, namely these neatly kept and productive little gardens round the labourers' houses, which are seldom unornamented by more or less of flowers." The man who dismisses flowers as unworthy of serious consideration is to be pitied, partly for his ignorance and partly for the self-deprivation, because flowers are a source of perennial delight. Moreover, a new generation is perpetually arising, to whom flowers are neither stale news nor irrelevant trivia but fresh and beneficent and wonderful. Something of that wide-eyed wonder is shared even by townsfolk when spring returns again, and the birds build their nests, and the wind sheathes its sword, and the flowers respond to Robert Bridge's roll-call:

> Pale Chlora shalt thou find,
> Sun-loving Centaury,
> Cranesbill and Sinjunwort,
> Cinquefoil and Betony:
>
> Shock-headed Dandelion,
> That drank the fire of the sun:
> Hawkweed and Marigold,
> Cornflower and Campion.

The British Isles

In idle moments it is amusing to ask idle questions, such, for example, as: "Where is the most beautiful place in Britain?" I confess at once that I do not intend to answer the question. Even a half-answer would displease those who live at Llangollen in Denbighshire, or at Arley in Worcestershire, or at Kilkeel in County Down, or at Bonar Bridge in Sutherland. Instead, therefore, of expressing an opinion, I shall state some facts, as follows: a plaque on The Brow at Kirkby Lonsdale in Westmorland says that Ruskin rated the view therefrom—across the River Lune and up to Barbon Fell—as one of the loveliest in England. Likewise Robert Southey declared that Lynmouth in Devon was among the three most beautiful places he had ever seen, not only in Britain but also on the Continent. A second poet, Sir Walter Scott, crowned Perthshire as "Queen of the Highlands".

A third poet—the mediæval Welshman, Cyndellio Brydydd Mawr—claimed that his own part of Montgomeryshire was peerless: "Whoso hath seen the fair and sunny land of Meifod, shall never see the like, not though he live till Domesday." A fourth poet, Mary Webb, persuaded many people that her native Shropshire stood high among the claimants for a *sans pareil* crown. A fifth poet, the author of *Lorna Doone*, hailed the North Devon sector of Exmoor as the fairest corner of "the fairest county of England". Dorothy Wordsworth fell in love with the Quantock Hills of Somerset: "Here is everything," she wrote, "sea, woods, wild as fancy ever painted, brooks clear and pebbly as in Cumberland." Rupert Brooke, on the other hand, preferred Cambridgeshire, if not for its landscape then at least for the intelligence and sympathy of its inhabitants:

> Cambridgeshire, of all England,
> The shire for men who understand . . .

Brooke would have approved my adherence to the ancient shapes and names of the British Counties and would himself have refused to acknowledge either the destruction of

Westmorland and Rutland or the creation of Powys and Avon.

Although tourism and aircraft have marred those regions, much of the visual beauty abides, and in seeking the finest of it we may recall our own favourites by sharing someone else's. I think, for instance, of Rosedale on the Yorkshire moors, where a walker hears only a breeze and the sound of his own breath while he strides through the heather. I think of the wooded skyline that greets a traveller descending from Netherfield to Battle in Sussex. I think of the dyke that switchbacks to Church Town at Middle Knuck in Shropshire, a land so far away from it all that the pilgrim comes close to everything. Have you seen Cornwall's granite coast, and the Dee at royal Balmoral, and Radnorshire's forests, and the oceans of corn on Salisbury Plain, and the No Through Road to Little Hampden in Buckinghamshire? Have you followed the unfenced lane from Inkpen in Berkshire to Linkenholt in Wiltshire, flanked by waist-high wheat? Have you made the long march over the Cardiganshire hills from Farmers to Llanfair Clydogau, once a Roman road, now partly a green one? Have you heard the sheep and the larks serenading a May morning on Romney Marsh in Kent? Have you admired the modest hills around Cow Pastures Farm near Whichford in Warwickshire?

It is indeed difficult to choose from such a litany of loveliness. I remember especially the track between Bix Bottom and Maidensgrove Scrubs in the Oxfordshire Chilterns, questing as a question-mark, a benefice of beechwoods and birdsong; the path from Charterhouse-on-Mendip to the Roman mines in Somerset, overlooking Wales; the high-banked lane (the roots of its trees peer down at you) from East Bergholt to Constable's mill in Suffolk; the miles of deep farmland and the handful of handsome houses on the meandering lane from Shipton Gorge to William Barnes's old rectory at Winterborne Came in Dorset; and Lancashire's Coniston crags. Once you have seen them, you will not soon forget the dun moor and the blue Tyne beyond the heights of Alston in Northumberland; nor the old road from Carlisle via Liddesdale to Hawick in Roxburghshire, a seclusion of sheep and hills and becks; nor the Foss Way following its own green footsteps past Jackaments Bottom in Gloucestershire. The litany is infinite: the peaks of Derbyshire, the Rhinns of Galloway, the Braes of Balquidder, the banks of Loch Lomond, the Spittal of Glenshee, the Kyle of Lochalsh, the Mountains of Mourne, the source of the Wye. And what of Cape Wrath in winter, of Evesham Vale in spring, of Dunkery Beacon in summer, of Savernake Forest in autumn?

Variety exists in every county, and often within small areas of a county. The climate varies, the weather varies, the dialect varies. While Aberdeen shivers, Penzance may perspire; while Portscatho sunbathes, St Mawes (scarcely four miles away) may blink at the mist; and an old Durham collier may sound partly unintelligible to an old Devon farmer. Are you, then, for the bracing north or for the soothing south? Is it seascapes you crave, or forests, or the placid charm of Rutland? Do you prefer the Cotswolds' stone, or Devon's cob-and-thatch, or Cheshire's gleaming magpie, or Norfolk's brick-and-flint? Would you choose a farmhouse in Holderness, or are you more at home in the spick-and-span companionship of a Surrey village? Truly this kingdom offers *multa in parvo*. Though he may never have ventured north of Lapworth, Shakespeare saw enough to convince him that "Britain is a world by itself"—a world embracing the Worcestershire fruiterer, Dean Forester, Durham collier, Caithness crofter, Pembrokeshire shepherd, Cornish tinner, Dorset marbler, Angus grazier, Severnside coracler, Cheshire salter, Channel pilot, Kentish maltster, Staffordshire potter, Lancashire spinner, Yorkshire weaver, Old Uncle Tom Cobley and all.

Some people maintain that nothing quite equals the sight of Hay Bluff as seen from the hills above Lingen, a sandstone rampart jutting its defiant Englishry amid the Welsh Marches. Some people hold a similar opinion of the lane that lopes alongside the stripling Severn *en route* from Plynlimmon to Llanidloes. Others gaze up at Skiddaw, needing nothing higher, or down at Loch Tummel, seeking nothing lovelier. Where, then, is your own outstanding beauty? Is it among the Cuillins of Skye, the steepness of Snowdon, the numen of Egdon, the trout streams of Hampshire, the stillness of Solway, the beechwoods of Buckinghamshire, the beacons of Brecon, the black peat of Fenland, the wild winds of Orkney, the green hills of Somerset? But who cares whether the beauty is outstanding or not? To some people the Essex marshes and the Leicestershire coverts are an earthly Eden. Others love best their city street, their urban avenue, their commuter cul-de-sac. Beauty cannot be separated from the eye of its beholder.

North Country

When Rupert Brooke sipped beer in Berlin he was seized with a sudden yearning which caused him to utter an ancient Greek lament: *"Eithe genoimeen . . . If only . . ."*

> Eithe genoimeen—would I were
> In Grantchester, in Grantchester!

Well, Cambridge is a famous district, and Fenland a fertile country, though one doubts that an Englishman would choose them as *sans pareil*, unless, of course, he had his roots there. If he did have such roots, and if they suddenly tugged him, he would liken Ely to Elysium, and the brash east wind to a zephyr out of Samarkand. Being, one assumes, a reasonable creature, such a man would on second thoughts amend his euphoria by saying: "Not everyone likes a flat landscape and a cold climate, but I do like them." If a third thought then occurred to him he would say either: "I like them because I was born and bred among them" or "I like them because I have come to know them, in good times and in bad." Thus it is that I, too, domiciled contentedly in North Devon, am occasionally seized with a yearning to be elsewhere. Though I may at the time find myself among the homely splendours of a Cotswold hamlet, or the lush pastures of Leicestershire, or Mary Webb's Salopian feyland, still I long to be in the north country. But where *is* that country?

Now the natives at Torquay start to shiver the moment they venture beyond Exeter. In Dorset they regard London as a kind of Pole Star or True North. Even in Oxford they tend to wear a scarf when travelling northward from Long Compton. But the men of Durham dream wistfully of the sunshine which, they suppose, warms the slopes of Derbyshire; and at John o' Groat's they find it difficult to believe that there really is any land south of Perth. As Einstein remarked, in another context, all is relative. So, once again, where *is* the north of England? For me the north of England begins when Nottinghamshire falls astern. I catch a closer glimpse when the Great North Road enters Yorkshire; and when at last the Pennines appear beyond Manchester, I have arrived. Yet the north itself must travel more than one hundred miles before reaching Berwick-on-Tweed, whose people and places vary from those of Burnley, even as Burnley varies from Grasmere and Morecambe and Chester.

Nurtured by ancestry and frequent revisitations, my own northern roots lie for the most part in Lakeland and Northumberland, and are deepest in that corner of England which for centuries was called Westmorland. So, while I stride across the Sussex Downs, or sit at home watching the red stags of Exmoor, I suddenly close my eyes and see once again the noble brow of Barbon Fell, and the churchyard at Kirkby Lonsdale, dancing with daffodils. I see also the wooded River Tyne, and the lane from Elsdon to Rothbury, and the green pastures surging round Flodden Field and those last few yards before England greets Scotland at Kirk Yetholm. No less clearly I see the windworn yet ever-welcoming little towns of Yorkshire (Sedbergh, Askrigg, Hawes) and the villages and hamlets for which they are a metropolis (Haygarth, Muker, Keld). I certainly do not fail to see the road from Whitby to Rosedale, blazoned with high summer heather, or swaddled in Christmas snow. What of Holderness, that sea-snatched solitude northward from Hull, where cliffside cottages are toppling into the waves while signposts point to places which have already toppled. Did you know that a part of Lake Windermere lies in Lancashire, the land of cotton and smoke and Gracie Fields? Have you ever compared Wigan and Burnley and Rochdale with Grizebrook and Thwaite Head and Devil's Gallop, where even one cottage comes as a surprise, and three create a built-up area? What of Holy Island, that sacred Northumbrian rock, where Aidan and Cuthbert led the good life, and a handful of islanders still try not to lead a bad one. And when you have had your fill of solitary self-communion you can drink a cup of good companionship at Dent Town in Yorkshire (the cobbled street is almost as long as a Long Vehicle) or at Firbank in Westmorland (the former parsonage enjoys the finest clerical vista in England) or at St Bees in new Cumbria (the famous school is near the sea). If you really do know the north country, you know also that its litany of loveliness is limitless: the green sweep of the Pennine Way above Edale in Derbyshire, the Welsh hills viewed from Malpas in Cheshire, the snow-posted lane to Middleton-in-Teesdale in County Durham, and so on and so on and so on to Alwinton and Humbleton and Cardunock and Gilsland and Garrigill and Hoseden. You are out of breath before you have begun to name even a small fraction of the vast whole. Yet the whole can speak for itself by repeating the words of a Northumbrian poet, John Story, who spoke for all northerners when he said:

> Is the cuckoo seldom dumb?
> And the wild bees, do they come,
> As of old, to sip and hum
> Upon Hoseden still?

But the north country is something more than a landscape. It is the home of England's homeliest people—homely despite a brusqueness that was bequeathed by ancestors who wrenched a meagre living from a stubborn soil; who either helped themselves or perished helpless; who dwelt far from large towns, and were strangers to whatever foppery passed for culture in London. Throughout the industrial north many people are as sheep, led and often misled by shop stewards; but among country places many people reap the rewards of personal independence and corporate seclusion. If, for example, you were to suffer a mishap at Ingram in Northumberland, the population—is it twenty or is it thirty?—would help to put you right. If you reached Darnbrook in Yorkshire you could spend hours—days, weeks, months—hearing nothing louder than curlews and a tractor. If you reached Bretherdale in Westmorland you would not find a shop there, nor a church nor an inn nor a garage nor anything at all except a few houses, and many sheep, and a plentitude of space.

For me the north country means waking up and feeling cold, and needing another two mornings before I adapt myself to the climate. It means sandstone cottages, and cobbled paving, and mountains, and spaciousness, and the tones of country talk from Ruston Parva to Port Carlisle: "Nay, thee mun be joking" ... "Happen t'owd fella put his shirt on't wrong nag" ... "Town planner or not, I told him, geet off my bloody land or I'll make thee wish thou'd never trespassed." The north country means snow in May, and fires in August, and rain from buckets, and wind like a razor. It means good talk and sociable silence. It means dollops of tatie pie and cups of perennial tea. It means "Blaydon Races" and Handel's *Messiah*. It means Len Hutton and John Peel.

The best of the north is a man's country, and the women know it, which is why they, too, are hardy and handsome and steeped in the skills of self-helping initiative. If you have ever savoured the solitudes between Pen-y-Gent and Horton-in-Ribblesdale; if you have ever walked from Clennel to The Cheviot; if you have ever heard the silence at Maulds Meaburn and the shriek of the Helm Wind at Dufton; if you have ever wintered on Holy Island, or summered at Stannersburn, then you know already that such places and the inhabitants thereof will not soon nor lightly yield to what we mis-name Progress. The northern fells and dales are still, in Milton's phrase,

Invulnerable, impenitrably arm'd . . .

5

To be a Farmer's Boy

Jeremy has two sons, aged respectively twelve and seven. The elder is already useful on the farm. The younger is learning to become so. I lately met them in a lane near their home. They rode tandem on a pony, each child wearing a jockey cap stuffed with newspaper.

"Not at school?" I asked.

"Us'm ill," replied the elder.

I stared, seldom having seen a bonnier pair of pink faces. "Touch o' bronchitis," the spokesman explained, trying, but failing, to cough. Then, perceiving my unbelief, he confessed: "T'aint us as is ill. 'Tis father. Doctor says he must bide in bed till Tuesday."

"So," continued the younger, "we'm away lambing."

"Just the two of you?"

"Uncle Jim's coming, soon as 'ee's finished milking. But father said to take a look round Five Acres. The ewes are dropping purty quick." He pointed to his young brother. "Tim don't know much about farming yet." After a pause, he half-consciously repeated the verdict on his own prowess delivered by his father to Uncle Jim. "But 'ee's shaping. The lad'll learn." By way of agreement—and although the pony had not stirred—the lad himself slapped its flanks, shouting: "Whoa there, damn 'ee!"

Curious to discover in what way our Comprehensive pedagogues were preparing children for their life's work, I said: "How's school nowadays?"

"Us don' think much of 'en."

"Oh? I'm sorry to hear that. What are you learning?"

"A project."

"What's a project?"

"So far as I can make out, 'tis something to do with doing something."

"Doing what?"

"Life in a 'undred years' time."

"A hundred years? But you won't be alive then."

"That's exactly what I told the teacher, but all he said was, 'Sit down and pay attention.'"

I could not help feeling that to guess about life as it might be in the twenty-first century was of less help than to know about life as it was in the twentieth century, when the children's grandfather ploughed behind a horse, and was rather poor, and took pride in his work. Nor was I persuaded that an illustrated lecture on Sex was likely to be needed by two boys who, even during their latency period, had assisted at lambing and were aware that rams and bulls and stallions took some part in the propagation of the various species. Rightly or wrongly, I felt that the old method—fumbling discovery, made in its own time—might prove less traumatic than a premature exposition.

Anyway, since the lane at that point was very steep, we all travelled on Shanks's pony, refreshed by the wind which dried the February dykes, by the primroses which shone like celestial parking lines along the verges, and by the moor itself, wearing the green livery of spring.

At the entrance to Five Acres I asked whether I could be of help. The two young farmers looked doubtful. "Have 'ee ever done this before?" they wondered.

"Long ago," I said.

"Then can 'ee tell when a ewe's near her time?"

"By the look of it," I replied, "they're all near their time. Let's go and see."

Halfway across the field the elder boy sighted three white dots. "Her's tripled!" he cried. Mother and children were all doing well. "No trouble there," we agreed.

Now if a ewe falls on her back when she is near to lambing, she may be unable to rise. We found just such a case, on the far side of a drystone wall, where a ewe had slipped in a hollow under the bank. "You must roll 'en gently," I was warned. So, clasping the legs while heaving the rump, we set the ewe upright, but only just in time, because she dropped her lamb before we had returned from the far corner of the field. Another ewe was less fortunate. She lay on her side, labouring in vain. My reputation rose considerably when I removed my jacket, rolled back my sleeves, and eventually enabled the lamb to enter the world alive instead of dead.

"You'd better tell Uncle Jim about this one," I advised. "She's too weak to stand up." Accordingly, they tied a piece of string round her neck, by way of identification. Suddenly the younger boy glanced at the sky, which had acquired a cluster of grey clouds. "Us don't want no rain," he exclaimed. "Rain is terrible bad for lambs."

While I was wondering whether to take the latest arrival back to the farm, Uncle Jim's tractor droned up the hill. By the time he reached us, however, the ewe had struggled to her feet and was licking the lamb. After a brief glance, Uncle gave a hopeful prognosis. "I can't see as either of 'em is any the worse, though 'tis as well you helped the youngster on his way." He turned to the boys. "Now, lads, nip along home and tell your Dad all's going fine. And don't forget to mention the triplets. There's nothing like triplets for curing a man's 'ooping cough." The boys rode away, and Uncle Jim said to me: "Those lads are shaping well. They'll soon learn. They'm both going to farm when they'm old enough. I reckon Jeremy's lucky to have a pair of unpaid hands. I pay my two fellas near as much as I earn myself, and even then I've often to work unpaid overtime to finish what they haven't started. Eighteen year old, both of 'em, and earning three times what I earned when I was twice their age. It don't make sense, Mister. It just don't make sense."

It is a pity that our urban educationalists take such a jaundiced view of W.H. Hudson's wise division of labour. "Go on," he wrote, "making your laws and systems of education for your own children, who will live indoors as you do; while I shall devise a different one for mine, which will give them hard muscles and teach them to raise mutton and pork and cultivate the potatoes and cabbages on which we all feed."

Blossom and Blackbirds and Cider

The apple tree stands in one of my paddocks near the brow of a hill eight hundred feet above the sea. Since the tree was planted more than half a century ago, it confirms Sir Thomas Browne's sylvan soliloquy: "Generations pass while some trees stand, and old families last not three oaks." At first sight the tree appears to have been bent by the prevailing wind, but a second glance shows that it is leaning *into* the wind. The lowermost bough grows parallel with the ground and only a few inches above it. As a result, the bole resembles a mossy drainpipe. Each year the veteran produces a fair crop of cookers.

Apple trees bear the most beautiful of all our fruit blossoms. By comparison the cherry looks too chaste. Before they have opened, the buds are almost red; having opened, they turn pale and might from a distance be mistaken for wild roses. The trees themselves are very resilient. Six years ago, for instance, I transformed the paddock from a tangled wilderness into a miniature meadow, useful alike for pasture and hay. I then set several apple trees, hoping to achieve a small orchard and with it the music which Ralph Austen enjoyed three centuries ago. "It is a pleasure," he wrote, "to hear the sweet notes and tunes of singing Birds, whose company men shall be sure to have in an orchard, which is more pleasant there, than else-where, because of other concurrent pleasures . . ." Among those "other concurrent pleasures" is a patch of bluebells at the foot of the old apple tree, which blends with the blossom above. Another and much larger patch shines from a wood fifty yards away. After a shower of rain the flowers do indeed hang like bells, but when you examine them closely you find that they are more like blue vases with an indented rim.

Anyway, I would by this time have achieved a small orchard had not a herd of heifers trampled the saplings, killing all save one. In the following November, while building a midnight bonfire of hedge trimmings, I dragged the fuel too close to the surviving sapling, which therefore became a Guy Fawkes martyr and ultimately a charred stump, scarcely three feet high. A few months later I noticed some young leaves on the stump, though the stump itself was so loosely anchored that a blow would have uprooted it. Horticulturalists tell me that the stem will never become a fruit-bearing tree. Human beings are not, it seems, the only creatures who may be blighted in infancy.

At the bottom of the wood, hemmed-in by hazel and ash and oak, stands a wild or crab apple, the progenitor of most of our apple trees. In more favourable circumstances the tree might have attained a height of thirty feet, but the struggle for existence among so many neighbours has kept it down to ten feet. The flowers and foliage of a crab apple appear toward the end of April, covering the boughs with a mass of blossom much visited by bees and other fertilizing insects. If the weather stays calm, the petals may last for several weeks, by which time the green fruits have developed, each crowned by the calyx of dead flowers. In September the fruit is ripe for making jelly. The apples—about an inch in diameter— may be either red or yellow. During October the leaves turn to a brownish gold, and the leaf-stem to bright red. Unless a gale topples them, the fruit will remain on the bare boughs for several weeks.

In a treatise which he wrote in 1570 Sir John Fortescue said that the English "drink no water, unless it be so that some for devotion and upon zeal of penance do abstain from any other drink". Two centuries later, John Philips wrote a long poem, *Cyder*, praising the Silurian or Welsh border apples:

> to the utmost bounds of this
> Wide universe, Silurian cider born
> Shall please all taste, and triumph o'er the vine . . .

W.H. Davies, another Silurian, likewise lauded

> apples, from whose womb
> Barrels of lusty cider come!

When John Clark compiled a survey of West Midland agriculture in 1794, he remarked: "The Orchards of Hereford-shire have long been celebrated . . ." It therefore comes as a surprise to learn that Herefordshire did not always appreciate its own fertility. "Many farmers," Clark reported, "consider cider-making as an intrusion upon operations of greater importance, and often wish there had not been an apple tree in the county." Devonians may retort that *theirs* is the first cider. Old men on Exmoor will certainly tell you that as lads they drank little else, unless it were tea. "In my day," they say, "we were all cider-born and cider-bred. Every harvester carried his own firkin of cider. It was as important to him as a handbag is to a woman. You might knock a tanner off his wages, but if you tried to reduce his ration of cider . . . well, a wise farmer didn't try to."

Meantime, I sit among the ruins of my orchard, debating whether to plant trees whose maturity I could never expect to see. But in May the tense ought always to be in the present because, like the present itself, spring has a habit of departing before we have fully sampled its arrival. So, while the sun shines on the newborn lambs and leaves, a blackbird sings from the venerable tree, as though to proclaim that apple-blossom time is the heyday of the year.

An Ace of Clubs

When the Oxonian Club was destroyed by enemy action in 1944, Mr Chips looked about for a new *pied-à-terre*. As a Gunner who had been invalided to a desk in Whitehall, he really did need a haven that was both comfortable and convivial. A fellow-Wykehamist offered to put him up for White's, but Mr Chips, whose private income scarcely exceeded £300 a year, decided that his purse could not support the subscription; and when the War Office rusticated him to the Hebrides, he no longer felt the need of a London base. So there the matter rested, until retirement from schoolmastering invited him to join The Castaways, a rural fraternity that was founded in 1830. The club's name is not to be interpreted as a refuge for shipwrecked sailors and social pariahs. On the contrary, the club was founded by a sporting baronet "for the convenience and entertainment of gentlemen of local standing". Every member had to be an angler, "able, if required, to cast his fly, at a distance of not less than forty feet, onto a silver salver". The baronet further insisted that members must tie their own fly "and be active supporters of the Tory Party".

The club used to occupy the whole of a Regency house in a quiet terrace in a market town, but in 1955 the struggle for survival compelled members to lease their ground floor to Amalgamated Prefabrications Ltd. Fortunately, they have kept the other three storeys and with them almost all of the club's original rules. Women, for example, are not eligible to join. Some years ago the youngest Castaway did suggest that a quorum of female subscribers would prove pleasantly profitable, but the Brigadier soon put a stop to that. "Young man," he warned, "I would remind you of what John Knox said. Or, rather, I would have reminded you if I could remember what it was he did say. It had something to do with a regiment of monstrous females. The point is . . . well, look at the Garden of Eden . . . they admitted women, and the whole damned show went to pieces."

The Castaways is exclusive insofar as it exercises the right not to include those whom it prefers to exclude. If Parliament should ever require the club to co-opt a quota of shop stewards and prize-fighters, its members will disband and thereafter meet in the manner of many others who have tended the flame of freedom amid the twilight of democracy. Formerly a society of sporting gentry, the club now attracts men from a wider field, including a Harley Street surgeon, a QC, a retired Dean, several serving officers, a sprinkle of landowners, three diplomats, and an MP who prevented Anglo-Uranian Motors from "developing" the Regency terrace as a multi-storey car park.

In earlier years the club, though not less convivial, was probably more audible, than it is today. The Silence Room, for example, bears no name above the glass-plated door. It does not need to. One glance at the occupants is enough to suspend the power of speech. In 1923 certain popular periodicals were banned from this room, ostensibly on moral and political grounds but basically because the rustle of cheap newsprint created a breach of the peace. The library contains an impressive collection of Victorian sporting literature as well as a complete first edition of Dickens (presented by Colonel Snodgrass) and a similar array of Thackeray (bequeathed by Bishop Pendennis). The principal painting is a local artist's impression of Queen Adelaide entering the club during a royal progress, when she graciously signed the visitors' book, whereof the page is framed beneath the picture. Last year, by way of experiment, a television set was installed and almost immediately removed, never to be replaced, for the QC—angered by a political broadcast—chucked an inkpot at the screen, exclaiming: "This once-great nation is now governed by the crude voices of coarse men!" The entrance to the club is sometimes daubed with the war cries of pacifist townsfolk, one of whom over-emphasized the Castaways' influence by scrawling "Hands off the USSR". Only last week the Brigadier scowled at "Trotsky In-Calligan Out". "Whoever wrote that," he muttered, "must have been a very comprehensive pupil." The old soldier then borrowed a billiards chalk and corrected the Russian spelling so that it read "Callaghan Out".

At its inception The Castaways attracted members from all parts of the county, rather like the club in George Crabbe's rural borough,

where to their friends in town
Our country neighbours once a month come down.

In 1898 the number of bathrooms was increased from none to
one; in 1967 the number of bedrooms was reduced from five to
three; and in 1968 the club deleted the rule which required
members to spend at least six months of each year within
twenty-five miles of the market town (but a property qualifi-
cation still requires them to maintain a residence in the
county). Although members never did adopt the practice of
black-balling, no one can join the club unless at least two-
thirds of the committee have approved him.

To enter The Castaways is to be greeted by many desirable
things of which many undesirable persons now disapprove.
Thus, instead of queueing for egg-and-chips members are
served by two elderly spinsters who long ago learned that the
MFH never takes beef when duckling is on the menu and that
the MP likes his claret to be lukewarm. For security reasons
or—as the QC puts it—in view of the spread of education,
members must now be identified before proceeding upstairs.
How does such an outmoded society contrive to remain
solvent? The answer is chiefly one of supply and demand, for
the club offers a service which its members rate as well worth
the sacrifice of lesser pleasures. Also, the club helps itself. Mr
Chips, for instance, is honorary secretary; an octogenarian
Paymaster Captain is honorary treasurer; a former High
Sheriff sells meat and vegetables from his farm at less than cost
price; and cadet members (admitted at the age of twenty-one)
undertake honorary roles as plumber, decorator, electrician,
and window-cleaner. The Castaways, therefore, is a place
where men of the appropriate Old School may for a while
forget the strident vulgarity of modern life; a place where they
may wear a suit of clothes without feeling over-dressed; where
cultivated conversation browses in many fields; where the last
heirs of a great tradition go down gallantly into the depths of
devaluation.

A Path Through Arcady

Having followed the track for fifty yards, we gave up, waist-high in nettles and briars. "A pity," we said, "because the map marks it as footpath." That was seven years ago.

This morning, while passing the track, I glanced wryly at the new signpost which proclaimed a public right of way. Noticing that some of the briars had been cut down, I ventured along the track, and found that it was no longer impassable. Downhill it went, skirting a patch of felled woodland on the left. Then it became a footpath, lined with bluebells and campions. Presently I heard the sound of a little river, invisible on the far side of a meadow on my right. On the left, meanwhile, the land rose steeply, and was thick with trees, some of them decaying because this sector of the plantation had evidently been neglected for many years. After about half-a-mile the land on the right closed in to create a ravine, and beyond it I saw the domes of other wooded hills.

Next, the river appeared, sometimes flowing over trout pools, sometimes spurting round its own curves. Now the wood on the left grew so steep that only a crawler could have scaled it, and only by worming his way among the trees, several of which were sprawling in grotesque attitudes. I noticed three that had been toppled by gales, each retaining just enough roots to keep it alive. One of them sent out lateral branches which stood upright like the prongs of a supine rake. At this point the path divided into an upper and lower route. The lower became flooded during the winter, but the upper—about six feet above the water—remained relatively dry, except where the trees provided a shower bath. After that, the bluebells and campions were joined by primroses, all shining in the sun; and after that, I halted to peer up at the biggest beech tree I had ever seen. Like the mast of a ship, the trunk disappeared among its own sails, which were young leaves that transmuted the sunbeams into shafts of silver light. Standing under the beech, I heard only the river and the insects and the birds. Moving on again, I saw that the trees on my left had given way to a wide bare patch whereon the bluebells resembled a lagoon.

Returned from its meandering, the river now lapped the side of the path, which soon reached a derelict shippon whose upper storey was supported by massive circular pillars. The building might have been a century old, perhaps older; but the original roof had been replaced by Bridgwater tiles, and several bricks showed among the cob-and-stone walls. The earthen floor was paved with dung; fragments of birds' nests drooped from the rafters; and the crumbling fabric revealed the chopped straw that went to make the cob. By modern standards the place was quite a long way from the nearest farm, for the men who built that shippon had no need to study time and motion. Cows, after all, are seldom in a hurry; and wise men never hurry at all unless during an emergency, which is why so many people have outpaced the art of living. On this path, by contrast, all things were actively at leisure. One white cloud loitered in a bright blue sky; the birds were as blithe as May itself; and a Friesian peered at me over the gate, as though she felt that even three miles an hour was rather too fast for comfort. All this being new to me, I thought of R. L. Stevenson's adventurous foresight: "Tomorrow's travels will carry you, body and mind, into some new parish of the infinite." True, I had scarcely ventured beyond my own parish; true also that the parish itself was far from being infinite; yet when I rested on a grassy bank, I almost fancied that it was the very place which had prompted Stevenson to remark: "You sit to smoke a pipe in the shade. You sink into yourself, and the birds come round and look at you; and your smoke dissipates upon the afternoon under the blue dome of heaven; and the sun lies warm upon your feet . . ."

The hills on the right were creeping closer now, and the land on the left rose higher still. If I had climbed that skyline, I would have seen even loftier hills, the Exmoor ramparts, stretching to their eastern apex at The Chains. The river was illustrating the persistence with which water finds its own level, twisting through long loops and abrupt bends, all the while eroding the banks. In some places the shore was wide, with a few weeds sprouting from the stones; in other places the water scoured the red earth. Twice the river veered out of sight before returning so close that the overhanging branches almost spanned it.

By this time I knew where I was and where the path would end, though the surface suddenly became so slippery that one false step might have sent me tumbling into the water. On my left the ground still soared steeply into a tangle of trees, some young, some old, each jostling for a place in the sun. At last the path became a track and then once more a path, this time turning away from the river, up a very steep meadow from which I looked down on a white farmhouse. In the next meadow the gradient slackened, the farmhouse sank below the brow, and the moor beyond it seemed to rise up and come closer. Looking back, I could see the path loping downhill through the two meadows, and the point at which it briefly became a track among trees. The river was hidden in the heart of the combe, just out of hearing, though in a rainy season I might have heard it. Now only the sheep were heard, and a lyric of larks, and from the invisible farmhouse the sound of a horse neighing.

At the far end of the second meadow I joined a narrow lane with grass down the middle, and then a track leading to the house. It had taken me less than two hours to explore the circular route, but more than seven years to find it. Henceforth I shall follow the path more often and throughout the year.

6

A Cockney in the Country

By her friends the late squire's daughter is called Bettina, but among the villagers she is "The Honourable". A few privileged people—the postman, for instance, and the baker—visit her so often that they feel entitled to refer to her as "The Hon". But no amount of abbreviation can lessen the lady's forthright foibles. Thus, she rolls her own cigarettes and has a singular as well as a plural salutation for all males—"Laddie" and "Chaps". Her working costume is jodhpurs, brown gymshoes, and the kind of check shirt commonly associated with lumberjacks. For the past decade her grey hair has been dyed the colour of an anaemic primrose. Despite a free and easy temperament, she is prone to what the Scottish lawyers call "suddenty", and in such moods she will use the word *swine* as a collective noun for everyone who displeases her (these include Oliver Cromwell, who once stabled his horse in the parish church).

The Honourable, then, is most unlike the widower whom the village calls Steve because he spent most of his life as a stevedore in the London Docks. Having retired last year, Steve forsook his home in order to tend an ailing father, likewise a widower, who had married the former squire's cook. Only Steve understands the traumatic effect of moving from the bustle of a street in London to the seclusion of a cottage in a wood. For the first week he went about in a state of apparent hallucination. Peering through a gap in the trees, he would say aloud: "Look at it . . . mile after mile of bloody fields and no

'ousiz. It don't seem natural." But Steve was as faithful as a son
as he had been as a husband. "Take it easy, old fella," he told
his father, "or you won't never live to be a 'undred. And if you
fail to score a century you'll lose your five bob bet. And you
never did like paying the bookies." Nevertheless, the strain
began to tell, even on Steve's vigorous physique. After
shedding half a stone in two months, he wondered whether he
could any longer endure the remoteness, the loss of cronies, the
absence of traffic and fracas and shops. He lost his cheerful
manner, and felt as tired at breakfast-time as at bedtime. Even
his flow of strong language dried-up. In fact, the best he could
manage was a terse: "I'm bloody dumbstruck." For the first
time in his life he consulted a doctor, who gave him some
sleeping-tablets, and told him to return to London. That he
did not return was due chiefly to the Honourable.

What happened was this: on his way back from the doctor,
Steve suddenly halted, muttered "Gawd luvvus" and then
questioned a roadman who directed him to the Honourable's
cottage, once the home of a gamekeeper. The Hon. herself
opened the door.

"Har you," Steve inquired, "the On?"

"So they tell me. Why?"

"Because I'm paying you a visit. Strictly social."

"Oh?"

"Your skeptic tank stinks something 'orrible."

"Those swine promised to mend it last week." The
Honourable sniffed. "Is the wind in the west?"

"I 'ope not, 'cause if it is they'll smell it darn the Old Kent
Road."

"Are you *au fait* with these tanks?"

"If *au fait* means what I think it does, the answer is Yes. I can
mend anything from a skeptic to a derrick."

"Then mend mine."

Such was Steve's introduction to high society, a rubric that
became a milestone. After mending the tank, Steve was invited
to mow a paddock. Never having handled a scythe, he viewed
the implement suspiciously. "If this is what Queen Boadiciea
'ad on 'er chariot, no wonder Julius said 'Seize 'er!' " He
looked closely at the warlike object. "What's this knob sticking art?"

"The handle," replied the Honourable.

"Stand clear then." Steve took a swipe and promptly fell down. "This thing's a bloody menace." He picked himself up. "Git back. Git right back." He took another swipe. "Blimey, I near sliced me ankle orf. You ought to 'ave a safety guard on this."

Three weeks later, however, Steve was mowing the rector's glebe and also the doctor's drive. After that, he took to drystone walling, which he mastered in less than a month, or at any rate well enough to secure employment and a sense of purpose. Today he is the Honourable's twice-weekly right-hand man, though not so close that they take luncheon in the same room, for Steve feeds in the kitchen, and the pair converse through an open door.

"Nice bit o' chutney this," Steve will say. "Who made it?"

"Fortnum," comes the reply, "and Mason."

"Are they local fellas?"

"They soon will be, if we get another Labour government."

"I don't like this fish paste, though."

"Actually it's caviare."

"It's more than caviare. It's bloody 'igh. Any'ow, I prefer bloater meself. By the way, what did your Dad git 'is title for?"

"For being born, Laddie. The original sinner got it for winning the Battle of Bosworth."

"Was 'ee in the RAF?"

"The first baron was doomed never to wear wings. Not even in heaven. And I fear that the last baron, bless him, will have some difficulty in getting airborne."

"Ah, well," says Steve, glancing at his scythe in the porch. "Time we clobbered them bleeding . . . beg your pardon . . . time we dealt with them naughty thistles." He whets the scythe with the nonchalance of a veteran. "And to think I once lived a civilized life darn the Old Kent Road."

News of the World

If I stroll downhill to a certain combe at about three o'clock on a Saturday afternoon I usually hear the sound of horse's hooves. The combe itself is narrow, sinuous, and so deep that parts of it are scarcely touched by the winter sun. A stream flows through the ravine, musingly melodic. Only two buildings stand there—a redundant chapel and a renovated cottage, each perched high above a track which eventually reaches a couple of gates and finally a farm.

Local people call this track "the Motorway", presumably because very few motors ever do use it, or need to use it, or dare to use it, for the surface is bumpy, the bends are sharp, and in summer the fairway is impeded by briars. At a specific nook on the track a cottager delivers a newspaper that has been collected from another cottager, living a mile away, to whom it has been delivered by a wholesaler at a town a dozen miles away. So ends the paper's journey of more than two hundred miles from London. The specific nook, by the way, is a gap in the hedge; and thither rides the farmer's son, a child as plump as the pony that carries him. Like most other children, the lad is—as the Samoans said of Robert Louis Stevenson—a *tusitala* or teller of tales. I do not know what tales he tells while riding to collect the newspaper, but I am convinced that their plots are exciting, for why does he approach the hedge at such a speed and then, instead of dismounting, snatch the paper as deftly as a train snatches the mail bag? Why else—having turned for home—does he spur his willing steed, crouching low over its flowing mane? Does he, I wonder, see himself as a courier, galloping post-haste with despatches for Bonnie Prince Charlie? Is he, perhaps, a General Custer, leading his cavalry against the Sioux? Or is he a potential Piggot, winning the Derby by the briefest of short heads? We shall never know, because the child will become a man who has either forgotten or is too shy to relate the visions that were granted him when he rode to collect his news of the world.

Townsfolk tend to forget that there are still places where a newspaper is both a luxury and a necessity, not delivered daily at the door but collected once a week, after a long journey in all weathers. Some years ago I used to visit a farm in the Welsh mountains, an eyrie so remote that no tradesman would venture up the miles of rutted track; only the postman called, and only when he had something to deliver. In order to ensure that the postman did deliver a weekly newspaper, the farmer's wife arranged for someone to send a card on the appropriate day. I remember, too, the celibate Sutherland crofter who, since he possessed no radio, and lived several miles from his nearest neighbour, relied on a passing friend to deliver the weekly newspaper. It so happened, however, that in 1939 the friend was called up just before war broke out. As a result, the crofter felt astonished when, a few nights later, a police car arrived, asking why his windows were not blacked-out. All such things being relative, the Sutherland crofter was better-informed than the Orkney crofters who, having neither police-men nor newspapers, continued to pray for King James II three months after he had been succeeded by King William III. Down in Devon the news of the death of Good Queen Bess did not reach the more secluded households until the Court had gone out of mourning. Something of this rural remoteness continued into the nineteenth century, as when the men of Penrith rang their church bells to celebrate the Battle of Trafalgar, not knowing that Nelson had been killed in action.

George Crabbe lived at a time when newspapers were beginning to permeate all save the very deepest country. Being a poet, he did not take kindly to the proliferation of prose.

> A daily swarm, that banish every Muse,
> Come flying forth, and mortals call them NEWS . . .

Nevertheless, he admitted that the media were on the move:

> I sing of NEWS, and all those vapid sheets
> The rattling hawker vends through gaping streets;
> Whate'er their name, whate'er their time, they fly,
> Damp from the press, to charm the reader's eye . . .

The more one thinks of it, the more one marvels at the people who escape the banes of communication by willingly forgoing its boons. Thus, among the wilds of Caithness I knew an elderly couple who remained blissfully ignorant of strikes and bombs until, every Sunday, their grandson arrived from Wick with a copy of *John o' Groat's Journal*. In Mary Webb's Marcherland a cottager walks more than a mile to collect his daily paper from a satchel beside the main road. In County Durham a retired farmhand walks two miles to collect his paper from a milk churn. My own newspaper is delivered at teatime by a farmer who leaves it in a box at the end of the drive. On Sundays, however, both the farmer and myself rest awhile from sharing the burden of Atlas.

Not a few countryfolk must take a boat in order to collect their news of the world, like the occupants of a Cornish cottage who row across the creek to an upturned dinghy in which the milkman leaves sundry household articles. I once made notes of the strange ways in which newspapers are delivered to people living far from a highway. My earliest note—it was really a memory—came from my childhood in north Buckinghamshire, where the horse-hauled bargemen earned a few coppers by acting as newsboys to households beside the canal. Sometimes the paper was chucked over the wall, sometimes it was stuffed into a box in the hedge, and sometimes the bargeman's child delivered it at the door.

Although it may sound like a mild joke, more than one reader has suffered the experience of the octogenarian cottager who received a copy of the newspaper which he had read seven days ago. When his wife said to him: "What's the news?" he replied: "Same as it was last Friday. It don't 'ardly seem worth buying the damned thing."

A Voyage in Noah's Ark

Glancing through the scuttle, even a globe-trotter might have hesitated to identify his surroundings. The climate was Madeiran, the sea was Aegean, the sky was Mediterranean. The chart, however, was English, for it showed that Noah's Ark stood within sight of St Anthony-in-Roseland, Cornwall's most mellifluous place-name and one of its fairest landfalls. Starboard shone the sea and a coast curving north toward Portscatho. To port the wide bay narrowed as it delved inland via St Mawes, a village whose many-coloured houses climbed from the jetty to a steep skyline crowned by a Tudor castle. At about three hundred yards from the shore I switched off the engine, allowing the boat to drift until, at thirty yards, I let go an anchor which, having dived into its own foam, held with a jerk. Slowly the boat swung round, with the stern resting six inches above the sand. It was not guesswork, so to gauge the depth and distance; it was old acquaintance, reinforced by memory of an error which had once left me high and dry while the lighthouse-keeper smiled down on what he took to be another landlubber.

In winter the small cove would utter thunderous echoes while breakers lashed the rocks, but now the ebbing wavelets were inaudible unless you came within a few yards of them, and even then they made merely a lisping plash. The sea, in fact, was so calm that it wove only a thin white necklace round the

shore. Through the clear depths I sighted five anchors which their unwary owners had lowered, not knowing that the flukes would foul a rusty cable on the bottom. In previous years I had watched people dive overboard, trying to retrieve the lost trophies from a cable too heavy to lift.

Already warm at seven a.m., the sun by mid-morning would become fierce. Meanwhile, holidaymakers were missing the best of the day by wondering whether the maid had forgotten their early morning tea. In solitude, therefore, I waded ashore, accompanied by the dog, who swam. We were both surprised at the warmth of the sand under our bare feet. It was firm sand, golden sand, and from it the tide had removed most of the litter with which the British imprint their own image. Topped by maritime pines, the cliffs above the cove were quilted with ripe corn and several meadows glowing green after a night's rain. Not a ship was in sight; all the shrill outboards were dumb. I did notice a car descending from St Mawes Castle, but the sound could not carry across the bay.

Very leisurely and forever fascinating was the tide's invasion of rocky pools and dripping caves. Each time a surge approached its final destination, the windless air robbed it of the necessary spurt, and it fell back with a sound midway between a sigh and a snarl. Then the invasion began again, the water exploring the cave as a tongue explores a tooth, tentatively, inquisitively, restlessly. After an hour of swimming and basking, I sauntered along the beach and among the murmurous caves while Noah's Ark rocked gently, slowly, in several feet of rising water. Before the gap could widen between ship and shore, I swam back, once again accompanied by the dog, who really was a sea-dog, able to clamber sure-footed along the narrow combing and to sit for'ard of the samson post, undaunted by spray.

There are moments when an amphibious life achieves the best of both worlds. Afloat on salt water, you are still within sight of dry land, which means that the anxious can soon be rescued from their anxiety, and the gregarious from their own company. By virtue of its simplicity, housekeeping becomes almost pleasant, for a two-berth boat needs very little dusting, and a bucket of water cleanses a multitude of stains. Likewise a Force 4 wind combines an assurance of safety with a sensation of seamanship. During the day the boat's motion seems as natural as breathing; at night-time it croons a sibilant lullaby. All round the clock and in every weather a sailor shares Cecil Day Lewis's kaleidoscope:

> Behold, the incalculable seas
> Change face with every cloud and breeze . . .

Food on board tastes good because the sea air is itself an apéritif. Relaxation comes easily because cruising tests the whole man, his skill at plotting a course, his dexterity at snaring a wind, his coolness at avoiding a hazard. Hilaire Belloc, who sailed his *Nona* through halcyon days and desperate nights, spoke like a mariner when he said: "The sea is the consolation of this our day, as it has been the consolation of the centuries. There, on the sea, is a man nearest to his own making, and in communion with that from which he came, and to which he shall return. The sea is the matrix of creation, and we have the memory of it in our blood. For the wise men of very long ago have said, and it is true, that out of the salt water all things came."

Sea and land certainly heighten an appreciation of each other, as, for instance, when you take your first long walk for several days, or row away from a car-crammed resort to the quietude of a cabin and the *camaraderie* of a cockpit. Some of the habits of a lifetime must be conquered when afloat, not least an inclination to argue about politics, which in any event become redundant when you enter a strange harbour on a thick night. Other habits may wither of their own accord, notably the illusion that news is important simply because the incident happened yesterday, or will occur tomorrow. Even wars and the rumours thereof seem less significant, not least because you can do nothing to avert them. Although the boat appears to be your friend, she is in fact neutral; and the sea likewise does not care whether you float or whether you sink. Needing, therefore, to maintain constant watch, you have little time in which to brood upon the crimes and follies of mankind. To live in a small boat at sea is to discover that you have lapsed into dependence on many unnecessities and have come to regard many necessities—exercise, fresh air, adventure, self-reliance—either as luxuries to be coveted or as misfortunes to be avoided.

Old Uncle Tom Cobley and All

Some of us were born in time to hear the last of the English folk songs sung by the last of the English folk singers. In or about

1914, however, the recitals became less common and more self-conscious. Ten years later the voice of the tractor was heard in our land, at the sound whereof the singers departed never to return. Certainly there are several skilled musicians who still do sing those songs, but effect is merely picturesque. Certainly, too, the English Folk Dance and Song Society has done much to rescue and revive the songs, yet—like the Beefeaters—the songs themselves are relics from an irrevocable past. Their language is often as outdated as 'thee' and 'thou'. Their ethos does not tally with our own blurred notions of right and wrong. In short, the songs no longer fit the singers. Yet, as I say, some of us can remember a time when the songs did fit the singers, or so nearly fit them that the words and music never sounded archaic. Sixty years ago, for instance, many farmers cut their hay with a scythe, children gleaned with a sickle, ploughmen drove a team, housewives made butter and bread and cheese. A few hinds still hired themselves for a twelve-month, and some of them lived at the farmhouse. Such men and women worked hard for six days a week, seldom taking what we would now call a holiday. They felt affection toward a good master, and loyalty to all save the worst. They were therefore describing their own diet when they sang:

> Bacon and beans, a bellyful,
> A bellyful, a bellyful . . .

They were recalling the itinerant tradesmen of their youth:

> It's of a pedlar, a pedlar bold,
> A pedlar bold there chanced to be . . .

They were speaking naturally, in their own tone of voice:

> As I walked out one morn in May,
> The birds did sing and the lambs did play.

As befitted an island race which not only ruled the waves but also maintained a fleet of coastal sailing-ships, those singers found nothing amiss in

> Overhaul, overhaul, let your jib-sheet fall,
> And put your boats to sea, brave boys.

That affinity is no longer possible, because farmhands long

ago discarded sickles and milk-stools and horses. Farmhands now plough by tractor, sow by tractor, reap by tractor. On a tractor they trim hedges, feed flocks, spray fields. How can such men sing spontaneously of milkmaids, sheep-shears, stooks and firkins? How can sailors sing spontaneously, of keel-haul, spanker vange, marline spike and topsail? They should sing rather of oil slick, overtime, sonic depth and radar. This does not mean that we ought never to sing our folk songs; it means only that we ought never to be fooled by them. Farmhands nowadays do *not*

> Rise with the sun to scythe, my lads,
> And sing in unison.

Having clocked-in after a leisurely breakfast, the modern farmhand may spend most of his working day alone, smoking cigarettes in an air-conditioned cab with a full-blast Radio One.

However, it would be quite wrong to suppose that our folk songs are concerned solely with vanished skills and obsolete junketings; wrong also to suppose that the old singers were sentimental prudes. Several of the ballads concerned unmarried mothers, as in "The Banks of Green Willow". Several of the singers regretted that they had not been born in time to heed Mr Punch's advice about matrimony:

> On Monday morning I married a wife,
> Thinking to lead a sober life,
> But as she turned out, I'd better be dead,
> The remarkable day that I was wed.

Cecil James Sharp achieved fame as a transcriber of folk songs at a time when they seemed likely to perish. But we should remember also Sabine Baring-Gould, the Devon squarson, who scoured Dartmoor in search of veterans who still remembered the words and music. Baring-Gould helped to collect *Songs of the West* and *A Garland of Country Songs*. Few people know, however, that his chief contribution to the subject was not the published works but the two manuscript volumes which he presented to the Plymouth City Library (some of the pages are mud-stained, and many were written in pencil). An Introduction to this collection states: "Our object was not to furnish a volume for consultation by the musical antiquary alone, but to resuscitate and popularize the traditional music of the English people. As, however, to the antiquary everything is important, exactly as obtained, uncleansed from rust and unpolished, I have deposited a copy of the songs and ballads with their music exactly as taken down, for reference, in the Municipal Free Library, Plymouth." Another and somewhat later transcriber was Alfred Williams, the self-educated Wiltshireman, who collected *Folk Songs of the Upper Thames.*

Attuned to the jungle rhythms of a Yankee tom-tom, England finds little joy in her folk music. Nevertheless, so long as the English language remains much the same as it is, and so long as Englishmen do likewise, so long shall the best of the old songs be sung:

> As I walked out one midsummer morning,
> To view the fields and to take the air,
> Down by the banks of sweet primroses,
> There I beheld a most lovely fair.

Up with the Lark

At least once a year I am up with the lark on a bright June morning. Summer being summer, and the weather forecasters being fallible, my alarm clock sometimes awakens me to a dull June morning. When that happens, I return to sleep. As a rule, however, the previous evening is a reliable guide to the following morning.

Up, then, with the lark: whether with the earliest lark, scarcely matters so long as you are stirring soon after three o'clock, while the world is still grey, and the dawn chorus sounds as blithe as in April. To hear the first bird and then, if you can, to identify it, is a source of unfailing wonder and deep satisfaction, as though you had not only witnessed the birth of a new day but had also assisted it. The sun seems to rise quickly. In fact, you can watch it rising, inch by inch, out of the sea or over a hill; but the radiance advances slowly. At five o'clock the moon still rides high, the coolness still deters the insects. At five-thirty a farmhand creaks downstairs, intent to do half a day's work before the sun starts to sting. Men have not yet unleashed their loud machines. Only the birds are heard, no longer in chorus but singing solo during brief intervals between feeding their brood. Then a lamb bleats, and a ewe answers, and the rest is silence.

One side of this garden slopes steeply to a small wood, and at about six o'clock, having surmounted a neighbouring hill, the sunlight touches the top of the wood, rinsing the strands of ivy until they glisten like seaweed, and burnishing the upper parts of trees until they resemble golden pillars. Slowly the radiance seeps downward, reaching all save the base of the trees, which remain shadowed among bluebells.

Standing on the lawn above the wood, I notice that the shadows fall away and are elongated. Estimating the spot where my own shadow ends, I descend into the wood, to measure the distance; it is more than sixty feet. The lawn itself is slashed by a single shaft of sunlight, six yards wide, in which the roses outshine their shaded sisters who seem not to have heard Ralph Hodgson's reveille:

> Now one and all, you Roses,
> Wake up, you lie too long!
> This very moment closes
> The Nightingale his song.

I pace to and fro across the sunny shaft, as a captain paces his corner of the quarter-deck; and at each turn, when I enter the shade, the temperature drops ten degrees. The atmosphere is pellucid, brushed by a gentle breeze, but at noon, the hills beyond the wood will shimmer in a heat haze. On one of those hills the lower half of a larch plantation glows black, while the upper half, which has caught the sun, burns like green fire. Higher still, the new-mown segment of a hayfield might be a beige patch on a billiards table. Most vivid of all are three foxgloves that have just come within the sun's range, and now gleam like pink and rakish nightcaps.

Strolling down the drive, I meet the insects at last—a bee, a wasp, and several midges—all flying low, as if the upper air were still not warm enough. From somewhere far away I hear a man whetting his scythe; for the rest, I am aware rather of mankind's absence than of its presence. Eden must have been like this, in the years before a Miltonic fruit-picker

> Brought Death into the world, and all our woe,
> With loss of Eden . . .

Cooing from the wood announces a pigeon, cawing from the hill announces a rook, and a cuckoo keeps on saying that these are the best moments of a year's life. The blackbirds are there, those masculine prima donnas, silverly sampling the perfection of their own arias. All the summer birds are there, each one defending a territory, feeding a family, and singing a song which some men translate as partly an ode to joy. The validity of that translation can never be proved by formal logic; it rests on George Santayana's intuitive syllogism:

> It is not wisdom to be only wise,
> And on the inward vision close the eyes.
> But it is wisdom to believe the heart.

Now at last the day has outgrown its infancy. At seven o'clock the once-grey sky is everywhere blue. Only the depths of combes and the crannies of north-facing hills are still in shadow. The sun has ascended from mildness to warmth, even as it will soon ascend from warmth to heat. One might say that the day has reached the most enchanting of all our anthropomorphic phases, the moment when an infant becomes an intelligible companion and a natural poet, not yet touched by the heat and burden of adolescence and maturity and the slow decline into twilight. Listening, I hear another cuckoo; watching, I see the grassblades gleam. Very soon the memory of dawn will fade; all too soon the afternoon will give way to evening, and evening to moonlight. Meanwhile, the shadows are shifting on the hills; the dew is glistening on the grass; the sun has touched the pond, transmuting it from grey-green to a blue as vivid as the sky. One wishes that the spell could last forever, and although one knows that it cannot, one continues to wish. Edward Thomas captured the magic:

> The glory of the beauty of the morning,
> The cuckoo calling over the untouched dew . . .

There is a sense of exclusiveness—almost of proprietorship—

in being astir while the rest of the world is still asleep. Hearing the birds, feeling the warmth, marking the sun's stately resurgence and the moon's gracious abdication, you feel as Traherne felt when as a Herefordshire child he stood amid his native corn: "The Skies were mine, and so were the Sun and Moon and Stars, and all the World was mine, and I the only Spectator and Enjoyer of it."

7

A Penny for Your Thoughts

Known to the villagers as Mrs Penny, Penelope MacBarra was born seventy-five years ago, her father being then a major in the Highland Light Infantry. At the age of seventeen she married a cavalry subaltern in the Indian army, with whom she lived happily until he was killed in action at Tobruk. Despite several acceptable offers, the widow never remarried. Her son, lately however, became a grandfather, and both of the married daughters have children.

Although Mrs Penny lives alone in a cottage on the edge of the village, she never feels lonely, for she visits and is visited by a few carefully chosen friends. Less intimately, the itinerant tradesmen are required to spend some time in the kitchen, purveying news of the world to Mrs Penny and her twice-weekly domestic help. Besides those human visitors, she enjoys the companionship of four cats, three spaniels, and an eighteen-year-old mare which she grooms and occasionally rides along the lanes. When cubbing starts, the local Hunt meets at her cottage, there to receive a stirrup cup that varies with the weather ("a wee dram" when the sun shines, and sweet cocoa when the wind blows). On such occasions the domestic help arrives at 6.30 a.m. to assist with the preparations.

Several years ago, after three local burglaries, Mrs Penny distributed most of her treasures among the family but retained a jewelled sword (presented by a Maharajah), a dagger (a collective gift from Jemadars), six silver cups (her husband's polo trophies), and a first edition of *Puck of Pook's Hill* (inscribed "For Penny from Rudyard"). Like many other widows of her class and generation, Mrs Penny was left with a comfortable income which has become so uncomfortable that she must continually devise new and niggling economies. She feels especially anxious about the animals. The spaniels, she told the doctor, will soon succumb to natural wastage, but the mare may outlive her, and the cats are still in their prime. "Never mind," she added, "so long as the dear strikers can play bingo in Biarritz."

However, you would be very wide of the mark if you supposed that Mrs Penny is also Mrs Blimp. On the contrary, she possesses such a flair for exposing fossilized convention that the rusty Right and the envious Left are alternatively delighted and dismayed by her pronouncements. Thus, while lunching at the Hall last week she remarked to a brigadier: "I feel so sorry for the Africans. When we governed them, they could take their troubles to a district officer. They lived at peace, and most of them were content. But now they're all fighting and quarrelling. It wouldn't be so bad if they still used bows and arrows. But they don't. We give them money we've borrowed from a Swiss gnome, and then they go and spend it on guns and aeroplanes." That went down very well at the Hall; but a loud hush arose when Mrs Penny turned to a political life peer, saying: "It's high time you were abolished." The company relaxed a little as Mrs Penny added: "We've already got one chamber of horrors. If we really must have a second, let's for goodness sake call it a senate. That'd do away with all those *pro tem* lordships." At a current affairs lecture in the village hall Mrs Penny clashed with a student teacher who had demanded a State subsidy for Women's Lib. "When my own girls got married," Mrs Penny retorted, "I said to them, 'If you want to be an imitation man, that's your own affair, but don't come running back to me when your husband discovers you're only an imitation woman.' " Strangers might suppose that Mrs Penny's frankness reveals a lack of compassion, whereas it reveals simply a dislike of false premises, muddled reasoning, sloppy sentiments, and excessive reliance on other people. The fingers of her own right hand are already bent by arthritis, and in a few years' time she must herself rely largely on other people. "I don't promise I shall grin," she predicted, "but by God I shan't whine."

Unlike most of her kind in India, Mrs Penny studied the native religions, which she prefers to describe as psychology rather than as theology. With her customary directness, she recently shocked a politician by saying: "In 1938 one of your comrades went strutting through Delhi, preaching what he called self-determination for the oppressed. I asked him if he could define *swarupa* and *trimurti*. He hadn't even heard of them. 'In that case,' I said, 'you've no right to be here, unless as a tourist or a commercial traveller.' " By an apparent paradox Mrs Penny has made such good use of *yoga* that she now combines it with occasional conformity as an Anglican; and this inner detachment draws much of the merely personal sting from her comments on men and affairs. "We were exhorted to love our neighbours," she reminded the vicar, "but we were not told that we must *like* them."

Despite decades of oriental climate, Mrs Penny remains slim, wiry, and pink-complexioned. She is proud of her size-three shoe and of her ability to read all save the smallest print without spectacles. When she is dressed for a formal function (she calls it a *tamasha*), her appearance evokes the word "handsome". When she dangles her gold watch-chain as a toy for a grandchild, one catches a glimpse of the seventeen-year-old girl whose fearless riding and good-natured frankness enchanted the very *pukka* subaltern ("I say, Pen, the colonel thinks you're no end of a sport").

With typical wry candour she views her own predicament as a relic of imperial pomp and civilizing circumstance. This became noticeable when an old friend, an Indian prince, called unexpectedly while Mrs Penny—gumbooted and wearing a sack over her head—was emptying the ash pan. In no way disconcerted, she said to her astonished visitor: "Had you called on me forty years ago, you would have been escorted by an aide-de-camp, and serenaded by my husband's piper. As it is," she gave a slight bow, "You find me in sackcloth and ashes."

High Summer

The word 'summer' comes from the Sanskrit *sama*, meaning 'half-year'. Like the year itself, summer is divided into seasons, low summer, midsummer, high summer. Low summer is scarcely more advanced than high spring because several species of migrant birds have only lately arrived, and the woods shine as they did in May. Midsummer is more spacious. From dawn till dusk the sun spans our waking hours and overlaps them with the long arc which George Meredith drew with a short line: "This was a day that knew not age."

High summer bestows almost a surfeit of colour and scent, for the corn is yellowing, the chrysanthemums are flowering, and the honeysuckle yields a second crop. An English summer day can be among the loveliest on Earth and better suited than any other to our temperate needs. Dismiss the climate as a joke, or curse it as a catastrophe, still you must admit that between May and August a countryman usually awakes to Mallarmé's welcome: "*La vierge, la vivace, et le bel aujourd'hui.*" Some people are so enamoured of summer that their urge to prolong it causes a mild amnaesia which persists until the evidence compels them to confess: "It must be nearly a month since the longest day." Much will depend on the weather. If June and July were dismal, we bid them good riddance, and pin our hopes on August and September; but if June and July fulfilled their promise, we remain true to them, and would, if we could, live with them forever. Returning home after a week's absence in high summer, you find that the sun and the rain have transformed the garden. A tardy petunia's single bloom has multiplied itself fourfold. The antirrhinums are in full flower, even among the cold north-eastern counties. A handful of rosebuds have become a bedful of roses. Wayside cow parsley or Queen Anne's Lace, whose flowers last month were no larger than a florin when you left, are now the size of a saucer.

Every season contains the seeds of its successor and the ashes of its predecessor. Toward the middle of July, for instance, the birds by their noonday silence announce that summer has reached its meridian. The deciduous trees wear a dark uniform;

only the holly enjoys a belated spring, glossy while the rest have
lost their sheen. Grass reaches its maximum height. Sheep are
shorn. Skeins of blackberries thrust tentacles across the lane, as
though to welcome early autumn. Everything looks luxuriantly
lush. Watching the cavalcade with unemotive precision,
science is careful to exclude imagination from its analysis.
James Thomson, on the other hand, blended fact with fantasy
when he viewed the ripening wheat and the plumping fruit.
"There is," he declared, "no thinking of these things without
breaking out into poetry." So into poetry he broke:

> 'Tis raging noon; and, vertical, the sun
> Darts on the head direct his forceful rays.
> O'er heaven and earth, far as the ranging eye
> Can sweep, a dazzling deluge reigns . . .

Thomson allowed, however, that the English summer may
unleash a very different sort of deluge:

> Down comes a deluge of sonorous hail,
> Or prone-descending rain. Wind-rent, the clouds
> Pour a whole flood . . .

Wet or dry, decay is a condition of rebirth, at any rate among
many plants. Half-hidden by undergrowth, the shrivelled
bluebells are making ready for their annual resurrection. The
daffodils are neither dead nor sleeping. Next year's leaf is
already an indenture on the twig. Despite preparations for the
corn harvest and a second crop of hay, the farmer's wife finds
time to cultivate her old favourites in a garden where Dorothy
Perkins rambles pinkly round the door, where honeysuckle
hides the wall of a derelict privy, where sweet-williams cluster
alongside asters and dahlias, where forget-me-nots weave a
summer sky for pansies and foxgloves. This cavalcade is seen in
meadows dappled with sorrel, campion, poppy, charlock,
hemlock, herb Robert, wild carrot, scabious, teasel, sheep's
vetch, and the perennial daisy. There, too, the last of the lambs
still run with the ewes, and hedgerows proffer a posy of roses.

Unlike most townsfolk, who regard July as a holiday season,
people in deep country, where agriculture is still the chief
occupation, regard July as a crescendo of hard labour and
anxious anticipation. In parts of Scotland the crofters are still

haymaking, and throughout Britain the arable farmers already know whether the grain crop has the makings of a heavy one. What they do not know, and seem unlikely ever to discover, is whether a drought or a downpour will dash their great expectations. Moreover, the harvesting is soon followed by the ploughing, both of which are made anxious because an excessively wet autumn will delay the sowing, and an unduly dry one will impair the germination of the seed. Farmers, in short, are not always so fortunate as Vergil suggested. They certainly feel no urge to share Walt Whitman's holiday hankering:

> O to sail a ship!
> To leave the tiresome sameness of the streets . . .

Work or play, high summer has passed the season's meridian. Sap rises less resolutely, leaves lose their lustre, lambs reach the awkward age. For the first time since February, winter becomes something more than an ephemeral dream. A cottager glances at the logs in his woodshed and then forgets them because the sun still provides both light and warmth; but next month he will quiz those logs more closely, saying: "The evenings are drawing in. We'll soon need a fire." Meanwhile, sufficient unto the season are the boons thereof, pressed down and overflowing.

Green Pastures and Iron Horses

Before the whole thing becomes merely a matter of second-hand hearsay, I wish to give a brief account of a small country railway station fifty years ago (I might almost have said thirty years ago, because the railway in 1949 was remarkably like the railway in 1929). At that time, of course, only an élite knew that a fondness for railways is a form of sexual sublimation. The train-spotting archdeacon would have blanched had you told him that locomotives symbolize libido.

Come, then, into North Buckinghamshire, just after World War I, when the scene is so rural that cars cause elderly cottagers to quake, and only the rather rich or the wholly commercial ever travel to London, fifty miles away. Of industry there is neither sight nor sound nor smell. The horrors of Milton Keynes are an undreamed nightmare. Farming rules the roost, and none of the farmers owns a tractor. Horses haul whatever is too heavy for men. Across this quiet countryside a bye-line meanders from a junction to a market

town. Of the few trains that use the line the least infrequent is a tank engine with two coaches which the countrypeople call the Steamer or "Staymer". Sometimes a goods train trundles by, trailing a guard who seems always to be either reading his newspaper or sipping his tea. Once or twice each day a non-stop train passes through, known locally as the Express ("Oi never milks Bella not until the Express goes by. She don't loike it if oi do. Maybe the whistle puts 'er in the roight frame o'moind").

Several miles up the line stands a Halt whose planked and roofless platform is raised a few feet above the ground, at a point where the line crosses a lane. This Halt is manned by a grey-haired factotum whose cottage overlooks both the lane and the line. It is a Victorian cottage and therefore well-built of good materials. Beside it are a garden, bright with flowers, and a vegetable patch, fertile with food. The only other building is a signalbox, the smallest in Britain and perhaps in the world, a kind of king-size doll's house. As a child living in Buckinghamshire, I visit this Halt, and sometimes take tea with the factotum and his wife, my grandfather having instructed them to keep an eye on the young railway enthusiast. How impressive it is, when, for my benefit, the stationman sets his head against the rails, saying: " 'Ere she comes. Doing thirty-foive moile an hour, oi'd say. Must be passing Percy's duck pond." Unbending his rheumatical spine, he consults a large silver watch: "One minute afore toime." Now he raises a forefinger. "Listen! 'Ear 'er?" With head tilted like a quizzical spaniel, I do indeed hear the never-to-be-forgotten chuff-chuff, followed by an imperious whistle which causes the stationman to say: "Sounds loike old Tom Gurney's cows 'as strayed again. Oi keep telling 'im, if 'ee don't soon mend thart fence 'ee'll 'ave a 'orrible accident, and it won't be 'is cows wart wins."

So, round the bend she comes, chasing her own smoke on a following wind. Off goes the steam, on go the brakes, and here she is, simmering like a stew while the guard lowers some steps, and up climbs a housewife (home from the shops), and down climbs a thatcher (bound for the Grange).

The bye-line is also a grapevine, transmitting many sorts of messages: "Tell the carter to expect three heifers and the doctor's sister-in-law prepaid on the late down special." "The four-twenty-noine is running seven late out o' Fenny with a hextra milk and one 'orse in a Great Western." Sometimes the messages are less technical, as, for instance, when the fireman says: "The vicar's on the warpath, way beyond Marston. It seems the Methodys preached a sermon against woine-bibbers in 'oly places. Th'old charp were fair fuming. 'Radical rascals,' he called 'em, 'hand-in-league with the Bolsheviks.' " But the stationman merely says: "Oi don't never argue politics, nor religion noither. Off you go, then." And off they do go, with a whistle and a snort, champing through fields and woods, so punctual that people living beside the line exclaim: "There goes the Staymer. Make sure the kitchen clock's roight."

How exciting, on a wild winter night, when the stationman—oilskinned and lantern-lit—comes out to let the Express through.

"Will she," I ask, "be doing sixty miles an hour?"

"If she is, Master Peel, you and me won't live to tell of it. Forty is quoite fast enough on this bend. Anything faster and she'd droive 'erself onto the bloody platform." A pause follows. "By the way, you don't never warnt to use words loike wart oi just 'ave. Anyow, oi don't often use 'em."

He enters the miniature signalbox (not even Master Peel is allowed inside), and presently a lever clanks, and the signal turns from red to green. Through the shrill darkness I see a cascade of inaudible fireworks, and after that the engine's yellow lamp, and after that a constellation of glowing coaches. Now she is alongside, shaking the timber platform. I can see the fireman, daubed by the glare from the furnace, and the driver, peering through a sooty port-hole, his left hand clutching the regulator. Next thing, only the red tail lamp is visible; then that, too, disappears, quick as a snuffed candle. Clank goes the lever, red shines the signal, out comes the stationman, click go the level-crossing gates, and through them passes old Tom Gurney, bolt upright at the reins of a cart. "Wart a noight!" he shouts. " 'Orrible," replies the stationman, adding: "And don't forgit to mend thart fence." Now he pulls out his watch. "Seven-thirty-six, and running on toime." He glances at my bicycle. "You'd best be nipping 'ome, else they'll wonder wart's 'appened."

What an age it seems, what an age it is—a different age—since the Steamer stopped at the Halt, and the Express rattled past it, and from the cottage a kindly woman called: "Station! Your pudden's gitting cold!"

Sense and Sensibility

When Vergil remarked that times change, he added an important consequence, namely, that we change with them: *"nos et mutamur in illis"*. In short, we are the children of our own era and can never wholly escape from it. Consider, for example, the average townsman's attitude towards the countryside: he regards it as primarily a playground to which he can retreat at weekends or during his summer holiday. This attitude is relatively modern, for although our mediæval ancestors admired the landscape, their written utterances seldom mention it at length. When William Langland dreamed his vision of England, he did not cite the hills and coasts; he cited the men and women, rich and poor alike, "working and wandering as the world requires"—and the first of those working folk was a ploughman. Admittedly, Langland's poem is a sociological tract, yet one might have expected him to say something of the landscape, especially since he saw it from the Malverns on a May morning.

Unlike Langland, William Camden and John Leland were topographers who explored a large part of Tudor England; yet they, too, eschewed anything comparable with Hardy's evocation of Egdon Heath or with Jefferies' ecstatic awareness of the Wiltshire Downs. Camden actually dismissed Exmoor as "filthy and barren", though the remnants of its dwindling moorland are now rated as the most beautiful part of North Devon and West Somerset. Likewise you will need to search many pages of Shakespeare for a piece of landscape-writing, and even then it will scarcely exceed five or six lines. During the eighteenth century that attitude changed, not least because the new turnpike roads had reduced the hazards and discomforts of travel. When Celia Fiennes rode through England, she leavened her account of crafts and industries with an appreciation of scenery. Even Defoe turned from his commercial preoccupations in order to admire a pleasant prospect. Nevertheless, neither he nor Celia Fiennes could conquer their Augustan aversion from the mountains and cliffs which we now value. Celia Fiennes was appalled by the modest summit of Edge Hill in Warwickshire ("it turnes ones head"). Defoe was daunted by the dizzy heights of Hampstead Heath ("a horrid air to breathe"). William Cowper lost his nerve while crossing the Sussex Downs (which Gilbert White called "majestic mountains"). Alexander Pope felt most at home among the domesticated country near Windsor, where he formed his boyhood notion of a spick-and-span estate.

By the second half of the eighteenth century, however, tourism had raised its profitable head (the word "tourism" first appeared in 1800, followed by "tourist" in 1811). In 1756 Dr John Brown's guidebook still referred to Lakeland's "dreadful heights" but was already half-inclined to admire them. Thirteen years later, Thomas Gray visited the district, still wary of the heights but already enchanted by "the most delicious views that my eyes ever beheld". As though anticipating Kierkegaard's "aesthetic man", Jane Austen reacted sharply. "Admiration of landscape scenery," she protested, "is become mere jargon. Everybody pretends to describe with the taste and elegance of him who first defined what picturesque beauty was."

Wordsworth, on the other hand, blended a love of landscape with a concern for the people who inhabit it. Granted, his *Guide to the Lakes* does carry a sub-title, "Description of Scenery etc", and the book's opening sentence does swim with the tide: "it was the Author's wish to prepare a Guide or Companion for the Minds of Persons of taste, and feeling for Landscape . . ." But Wordsworth insisted that the land is not primarily a peep-show for tourists; it is primarily a place where men and women earn an arduous livelihood by helping to feed their compatriots. He therefore advised the lady from South Kensington to acquaint herself with the rudiments of geology (which shaped the land) and with the outlines of history (whereby forests were cleared, feudal manors were established, commons were enclosed, cities were expanded, and Britain acquired its industrial or piebald appearance). Wordsworth's poetry offers the same advice. Thus, although the first book of *The Prelude* praises "the all-sufficing power of solitude", the second book entitled "Love of Nature leading to Love of Man", is Wordsworth's heroic self-analysis; not, indeed, forsaking Nature, nor forsaken by it, yet paying greater attention to "how men live, even next-door-neighbours, as we say".

Even in 1820, however, a large number of visitors to Lakeland were not at all "Persons of taste, and feeling for landscape". On the contrary, Wordsworth deplored the effects of tourism, and especially the tide of hotels and "holiday cottages". He foresaw clearly what would happen if the immigrants were allowed to enlarge their buildings and to erect new ones. "It is," he wrote, "much to be wished that a better taste should prevail among these new proprietors; and, as they cannot be expected to leave things to themselves, that skill and knowledge should prevent unnecessary deviations from the path of simplicity and beauty along which, without design and unconsciously, their humble predecessors have moved. In this wish the author will be joined by persons of pure taste throughout the whole island, who, by their visits (often repeated) to the Lakes in the North of England, testify that they deem the district a sort of national property, in which every man has a right and interest who has an eye to perceive and a heart to enjoy."

Modernity has mocked Wordsworth's modest expectations. Lakeland is now "a sort of national property" in which every man has the right to increase the traffic jams, to multiply the garages, to extend the housing estates and to 'develop' derelict barns into weekend cottages. Lakeland in summer is a car-crammed cacophony. Every one of its towns and almost all of its villages have been disfigured by new houses that were built not for long-term occupation by natives but for short-term occupation by tourists and retired strangers.

8

A Stately Home

Four lines of verse are sometimes more vivid than four pages of prose. Consider this:

> The stately homes of England!
> How beautiful they stand,
> Amidst their tall ancestral trees
> O'er all the pleasant land.

Now consider this:

> The stately homes of England!
> How beautiful they stand,
> To prove the upper classes
> Have still the upper hand.

The first of those stanzas was written by Felicia Hemans, who achieved a brief popularity during the early years of the nineteenth century; the second stanza was written by Noel Coward during the 1930s; and both of them described a Victorian aristocracy which seemed invulnerable. But taxation began to erode the great estates during World War I, whereafter an ever-increasing exaction caused some of the stately homes to crumble and others to become unoccupied except for a few rooms. When those homes were built, the majority of Englishmen assumed that widespread poverty was unavoidable. Today, by contrast, the national conscience is in every sense more tender. Among some people it is so tender that they would sell anything—from a Corot to a cathedral—if by so doing they could distribute a loaf to every member of the community. But we are not here concerned to debate the matter. You either approve or disapprove a Welfare State wherein a relatively few people can, if they choose, live a life of cultivated leisure in an historic and beautiful house among spacious and well-kept parklands.

Genes, like stately homes, are inherited by chance. Thomas Hardy, a stonemason's son, chanced to inherit the kind of genes which enabled him to rise high on his own private enterprise. It was therefore from personal experience that he viewed both the crest and the trough of destiny's chanceful wave: "I am," he declared, "against the taxing of the worthy to help the masses of the population who will not help themselves when they might. Opportunity should be equal for all, but those who will not avail themselves of it should be cared for merely—not be a burden to, nor the rulers over, those who do avail themselves thereof." By disregarding that common sense, the so-called Welfare State has caused many great houses to face a dilemma: they must either fall to bits, or be sold as commercial premises, or become museums which the public pays to enter. I am not alone in feeling a sense of unease— almost of trespass—whenever I do pay to inspect another man's house. Nevertheless, I approve the arrangement because it may ensure that the house is inherited by heirs who will likewise rescue it from a less desirable fate. There are two ways in which a private residence may be converted into a partly public one. The first or wrong way is to turn the place into a holiday camp, a loud jamboree, a series of sideshows and bargain basements, the profitable plaything of accountants and publicists. The second or right way is the one followed by a friend of mine who inherited a stately home in Leicestershire, which he has preserved as a family home, parts of which are shared by the public, his guests. I emphasize the word "guests" because it is the word that appears on the various signposts and announcements. Moreover, my friend and his wife mingle with their guests, like hosts who wish to see that the party is enjoying itself fully and fittingly. Among the outdoor attractions at this house is the finest $10\frac{1}{4}$ inch gauge passenger-carrying steam railway in Britain—one-and-a-half miles of it, with stations, tunnel, and automatic level crossings. Through woods it goes, then across meadows, and finally to a large lake where passengers embark in scale-model cruising liners. Inside the house the guests may see splendid furnishings, memorable paintings, historic heirlooms; yet at no time are they harried by warning notices, roped-off areas, and yawning guides. The necessary precautions are so unobtrusively efficient that hospitality reaps its own reward, and the visitors may say, as Francis Bacon said: "It is a reverent thing to see a Castle or other ancient Building that is not in decay."

Many motives lead us to visit such places. We admire the architecture of the house and the landscaping of the park and gardens for patrons who could still afford to employ architects who could still understand how to build handsomely, fittingly, and durably. Forgetful, perhaps, that the earlier occupants of those houses lacked a bathroom and a water-closet, we find our imagination stirred by the splendour and precision of everyday life; the majestic major-domo and the tremulous tweenie, the appropriate costume for the punctual occasion, the clatter of cabriolets on cobbles, the silverware gleaming in candlelight, the fact that Britain ruled not only the waves but also a large part of the earth. In short, we share our forefathers' greatness, to an extent that was formerly beyond the range of all except the few who enjoyed an *entrée* into such houses.

No one can foretell what will happen to Britain's stately homes. Some of them may survive as my friend's has survived. Others may become offices, or ruins, or so-called cultural centres. A few may remain the wholly private homes of rich aliens. But one thing at least is certain—those of us with a sense of history and an eye for beauty feel grateful to all landowners who have followed the example of Lord and Lady Gretton of Stapleford Park near Melton Mowbray in Leicestershire.

The Golden Valley

The map marked a place called Arcadia, as though to endorse John Masefield's claim that his native Herefordshire was "a country of exceeding beauty and strangeness". The name Arcadia certainly reinforced my own long-held belief that the Golden Valley is indeed an English equivalent of Arcady, a region of the Peloponesus which the Greeks chose as their idyllic countryside.

The valley's name is both evocative and misleading because the local river, the Dore, was at one time called the *Our*, a Saxon corruption of the Welsh *dwr*, water. But when the Normans arrived, they assumed that 'Dore' was a Saxon corruption of the French *d'or*, meaning *golden*. Golden therefore the valley became, and golden it was when I saw it, new-minted of things more precious than metal, for there shone the cornfields, some reaped, some standing; there shone the orchards whose fruit had already acquired a tan; there shone the sun, coaxing and commanding the utmost glint from amber thatch, russet stubble, reddish soil, and the blue streams which fed the Dulas Brook. North-west from Ewyas Harold to a point near Dorstone, the wide valley justified its glittering name while midges revolved in shafts of sunshine that were made even more golden by the dusty chaff. Wayside hedgerows clutched at golden straw dropped there by high-piled harvest carts swaying down narrow lanes. Even the tawny Herefordshire cattle looked as if they, too, might at any moment be transmuted into the same sunbaked substance.

Most of the houses in the valley were built long ago, and their gardens glowed with flowers. Seldom had I seen so much honeysuckle; never so many of the last roses of summer. Driving at twenty miles an hour, or walking at three, I spent the whole day happily lost in a maze because the wise County Council does not waste money on signposting lanes that are used only by natives who have no need to be told the way home. Through Longtown I went, and Bacton and Vowchurch and St Margarets; always with the Welsh mountains on one side and the Hay Bluff nearby, jutting out like the paw of an enormous lion. It was difficult to believe that this quiet countryside had for centuries been harried while the English subjugated a neighbour whom they could not allow to remain as a thorn in their side. The map told the story in a few words: Cwmdulas, Maes-coed, Llancillio, Ty-bach, Bagwyr Llidiart. Alone, then, in a tangle of footpaths and lanes, I began to wonder whether anybody still lived there. Tractors I heard, bumping home with the harvest, and sometimes a child calling and a dog barking, but nothing else. At one small church with one small bell a signboard said: "Parishes of Clodock St Margarets with Michaelchurch Escley and Newton." Yet the old people could remember when every parish maintained its own priest.

From time to time I passed the kind of picture-postcard cottage which deludes us into thinking that in it we could discard all our anxieties, living lightheartedly forever, as they did in the Forest of Arden. Several of the cottages hid so shyly among trees that my surprise at seeing them amounted to a physical sensation. After two hours' walking I did glimpse someone, but he was three fields away, mending the roof of a barn. For the rest, it was uphill along heathy tracks and then downdale into meadows, cornfields, orchards, and the shimmering sibilance of the woods which enchanted Mary Webb in her own corner of the Marcher Country:

> Let us away, out of the murky day
> Of sullen towns, into the silver noise
> Of woods where every bud has found her way
> Sunward, and every leaf has found a voice.

Ought one to publicize such peaceful privacy? Are there not cars enough, without hearsay sends them even deeper into the remnants of rural solitude? But take heed, for the secret places of the Golden Valley add a warning to their welcome—walkers and horsemen, yes; cyclists, perhaps; cars, never.

History haunts this seemingly uneventful Arcady. At Bacton (where a house was called Paradise) lived Blanche Parry, maid-of-honour and lifelong friend to Queen Elizabeth I. Although Mistress Parry's home, New Court, has been rebuilt, her epitaph proudly recalls the old mansion and her own career as a courtier: "I Parrychys dorter of New Covrte borne, That treynyd was in pryncys covrts . . ." They say that the altar cloth, which has been preserved under glass, was made by Blanche Parry, to her own design of birds, animals, insects, flowers and two people in a boat. This faithful servant went blind, and her death at the age of eighty-two deeply grieved the Queen, not least because, as the epitaph says, both women were spinsters: "Wythe maeden Quene, a maybe dyd ende my lyffe."

The village of Ewyas Harold was surnamed by William the Conqueror's nephew at a time when the district reared many sheep (Ewyas is a Welsh word via the Latin *ovis, sheep*). In 1147 Harold's son, Robert, founded the Abbey Dore, which lies in the heart of the valley, surrounded by fields and woods. Plundered after the Dissolution, and then allowed to decay, the site was given by Henry VIII to the Scudamore family. In

John Aubrey's day the local people were still pillaging the statues. "A mower," he reported, "had taken one of the armes to wett his syth." In 1632 some of the ruins were restored by the first Viscount Scudamore, who commissioned a Hereford-shire man, David Addams, to build the present tower above the inner south transept. The church was then re-roofed with 204 tons of Herefordshire oak which cost (in modern currency) less than two pence per hundredweight. Re-consecrated on

Palm Sunday 1634, the anniversary of the Viscount's birthday, Dore is one of the very few Cistercian churches that are still used regularly for worship.

Entering the abbey from fierce sunlight, I was greeted by coolness and the piety of the centuries of farmfolk who in their joy came to give thanks and in their sorrow to seek comfort. "Come unto me all that travail and are heavy laden, and I will refresh you." So says the Prayer Book, so says the Abbey Dore, and so after its fashion says the Golden Valley.

News from the Parish Pump

Ask a townsman to name the parish in which he resides, and he will probably say: "Name the *what?*" If you question him further and ask the name of his parish priest, he will regard you either as a crank or as a crook. In deep country, on the other hand, every villager knows the name of the local parson and very likely the name of the saint to whom the parish church is dedicated. In short, most countryfolk equate their parish with their village. The Church of England may be dying, but its legacy lingers on, and not simply as a mystique, for Thomas Hardy, an anti-Christian, believed that the parish churches are a unique bulwark against national decadence. "One may ask," he wrote, "what other purely English establishment than the Church, of sufficient dignity and footing, with such strength of old association, such scope for transmutability, such architectural spell, is left in this country to keep the shreds of morality together?"

Derived from the Greek *paroika*, *group of people*, the parish was the earliest administrative unit of Christianity. By the end of the Dark Ages it had become a synonym for any settlement containing a church and a priest. Less than two centuries ago Sir William Blackstone could still define a parish as "that circuit of ground in which the souls under the care of one parson or vicar do inhabit". Most of the Saxon churches were sited and built under the aegis of the nearest bishop; but when the demand exceeded the supply, it became usual for lords of a manor to build and endow their own demesne churches, which the bishop then consecrated, albeit at some cost to his authority because he allowed the lay founders to appoint their own incumbents, and the incumbents to collect a tithe (tenth part) of the parochial farm produce.

Most of the early-mediæval parish priests were rectors (Latin *rego, I rule*). Unless a rector disgraced himself, he held the parsonage for life. However, as the demand for churches increased, the bishops encouraged lay founders to present their churches to a monastery whose abbot or prior then became the rector, though he generally appointed a deputy or *vicarius* to serve the church. These vicars ultimately obtained an ordinance (whence 'ordination'), granting them security of tenure and, at least in theory, one-third of the parish revenue. By the end of the Middle Ages more than a quarter of the English rectories had become vicarages.

The size and shape of parishes varied greatly. Some were tiny, like that of St Martin in Exeter, which covered less than two acres; others were vast, like that of Clun in Shropshire, which covered more than 350 square miles. At Cheriton Bishop in Devon the parish boundaries almost tally with those of an estate that was held by a Celtic nobleman, Hyple, during the reign of the Emperor Hadrian. If a man's land overspilled into another parish, and if he then built a house on the border, the results might prove comical, as in Buckinghamshire, where the boundary between Prestwood and Great Hampden bisects the bedroom of a farmhouse. Some priests still observe the custom of beating the parish bounds, or, rather, of beating the backsides of the parish boys who, as a result of that symbolic chastisement, would remember the boundary and be able to define it in cases of doubt or dispute.

The mediæval parish clerk was an important person, usually in minor orders, charged with supervising church worship and parish education. In 1442 King Henry VI granted a charter to the parish clerks of the City of London "for that special devotion they especially bore to Christ's glorious confessor St Nicholas . . ." On the saint's feast day the brethren of the Worshipful Company of Parish Clerks take Holy Communion before meeting in common hall "to contine the tradition of some seven centuries of their existence". After the Reformation the parish clerk was always a layman, concerned chiefly with parish relief and other local charities. George Crabbe, himself a country parson, described a Suffolk parish clerk in 1810:

> sober, chaste, devout, and just,
> One whom his neighbours could believe and trust.

The parish clerk had to be at least twenty years old and of good repute, "sufficient for reading and writing and also for his competent skill in singing" (the Beadle of the Company of Parish Clerks carries a staff whose silver head is inscribed with a tune from an open psalter). Until 1921 a parish clerk held office for life and could be dismissed only after legal action. Today he serves under contract to the parson and the parochial church council.

Although the parish ultimately became a vehicle of taxation by the Crown, it continued as an ecclesiastical unit, unlike the secular or civil parish, a Victorian device, for which a separate Poor Rate could be levied. At their inception the parish councils were empowered to manage all parochial lands and buildings, such as commons and village halls; to provide public baths and libraries and to levy a special rate for that purpose; to buy land for allotments and to maintain, close, or divert public rights-of-way. In hamlets and small villages without a parish council, a meeting of rate-paying parishioners may undertake the work of a parish council. These *ad hoc* meetings seldom fail to achieve a quorum, for the true countryman would rather be governed by other countrymen than by distant strangers. At present, despite the spread of urban bureaucracy, the parish council still plays a useful role in rural life. Its members are known personally to the electorate, and its business is rarely impeded by the political rancour that has infected many county councils since their members were paid by the hour and at so-much per mile.

Riding Down the Lanes

The latest addition to my ménage is Tim, a grey pony. His owner, having lately moved house, intended to sell him, not without regret, because the animal had endeared himself to all the family. Pending the sale, Tim came as a non-paying grazer of my own grassland. After a few days I, too, regretted that he must be sold, perhaps to a neglectful buyer. I therefore invited him to live here permanently, or at any rate for so long as we both approved the arrangement. On first arriving, Tim was inspected by Tinker the cat and by Jack the Russell, who assessed him as a large and malformed member of a strange species. Tim, for his part, merely looked down his nose at the midgets. In less than an hour, however, the tension had eased, and now they are all such good friends that they meet one another at the fence, where the cat performs feats of conspicuous bravery within a yard of the pony's hindlegs, though never nearer than a yard. Not to be outdone, the dog sometimes chews a blade of grass but quickly spits it out as unfit for canine consumption. At present the trio are basking full-length in the sun, with Tinker's tail almost touching Tim's. They make a pleasant sight, less common yet not less real than Nature's bloodstained tooth and claw.

Since I happen to be six feet tall, I cannot mount Tim without seeming to be too near the ground. This troubles me not at all, for on Exmoor—as in parts of Ireland—it suffices to keep one's stirrups clear of the mud. Given that clearance, any rider can enjoy many of the pleasures of horsemanship. Leigh Hunt was right when he said: "Horseback is the noblest way of being carried." Riding a horse may in some degree be likened to riding a bicycle. True, you do not need to steer so sedulously nor to balance so constantly, yet even the steadiest steed may shie and thereby discard the rider who has failed to grip with his knees. True also that on a horse you do not need to change gear, yet even the laziest rider must support his own spine. Moreover, no horse is so meek that it will not defend itself against a bad or a callous rider. John Gilpin, you remember, paid the price of his unequestrianism:

> His horse, who never in that sort
> Had ridden been before,
> What thing upon his back had got
> Did wonder more and more.

When wonder gave way to astonishment, and when astonishment gave way to resentment, the horse bolted and went on bolting until the startled spectators, assuming that Gilpin was a criminal, raised the hue and cry:

"Stop thief! Stop thief!—a highwayman!"
Not one of them was mute;
And all and each that passed that way
Did join in the pursuit.

Like a cyclist, the horseman can peer over hedges; unlike a cyclist, he needs not dismount in order to halt. Like a pedestrian, he can observe the countryside at leisure; unlike a pedestrian, he can quicken the pace by prodding the ribs. Cyclists and pedestrians, however, must propel themselves, whereas horsemen have only to collect themselves. While cyclists tend to become obsessed by the act of self-propulsion, and while pedestrians may sleep in the shade, a horseman who proceeds at walking pace is unlikely to fall asleep and can never become obsessed by the speed of his progress. Above all, a horse and its rider can share a rapport which is denied both to cyclists and to pedestrians. Like human beings, a horse responds to intimacy and old acquaintance. If, for example, a child is left too much in the care of a nursemaid, he will fail to develop the affection which another child feels toward his parents who minister to all his needs. Just so, the man who hands his horse to a groom will never achieve the empathy that is shared by the man who feeds, waters, grooms and saddles his horse.

When Tim takes me leisurely down the lanes, I am reminded that during my childhood a car was seldom seen in deep country. The squire might own one, and so might the doctor, but the vehicles disliked stiff gradients, and were apt either to boil or, like a mule, to remain stubbornly immobile. Arriving at a small country railway station, townsfolk in those years discovered that the infernal combustion engine was by no means ubiquitous. "Sorry, Sir," the porter-cum-signalman would say, "we've no taxi here. George does sometimes oblige with his Ford, but he's away haytiming. You'd best bide another half-hour. Old Will's wife usually passes then. Maybe she'll take you in the wagon. Even so, you'll have a three-mile walk from the Cross Keys. Still, it's just the morning for a stroll. I'll give you a tip, though. Watch out when you leave Will's Wood. There's a skittish bull roaming the next field. In fact, Will only came out of hospital last week."

Since few cars venture up these one-in-three hills, and since none of the lanes is wide enough to take a large lorry, my own rides are truly rural, the sort which Robert Bridges prescribed as a panacea for all save the direst disease:

> Riding down the country lanes:
> The larks sang high.
> O heart, for all thy griefs and pains
> Thou shalt be loth to die.

Although the level sectors hereabouts are seldom longer than three hundred yards, they do allow the pony and myself to jog our livers with a trot; and by avoiding the steepest routes, I am relieved of the need to get down and walk. Lest non-horsemen regard me as too great a burden, I would remind them that Tim resembles a Welsh cob, and that the word *cob* is used of any sturdy and short-legged horse. All such animals are well able to carry riders heavier than myself. One of our farmers goes shepherding on his young son's pony; another rides a pony to and from the nearest village. When cubbing starts, I shall certainly ride to watch the Meet, dwarfed but not daunted by six-foot farmers on weight-carrying monsters.

Paying to Hear the Blackbirds

How pleasant it is to discuss a controversial question in an unprovocative way; that is, by confining oneself to a statement of verifiable facts which neither malice nor misunderstanding can deny. My question is this: are there any regions of England which regularly enjoy a whole day's respite from the sound of aircraft? That question is not an idle one. On the contrary, millions of Britons are asking the same thing albeit silently and without hope of receiving an affirmative answer. It so happens that my own lawful occasions take me to many places from Land's End to John o' Groats and from the Mountains of Mourne to the Firth of Forth; and in the course of those travels I follow Captain Cuttle's advice to make notes or *obiter scripta*. Glancing through the notes the other day, I was dismayed by their frequent reference to noise in general and to aircraft in particular. Thus, I lately spent two days revisiting my old home in the Chiltern Hills, and at the end of the tour I noted: "For thirty-five years I lived here in peace. Now, alas, aircraft rumble day and night, sometimes so loudly that conversation becomes impossible. The woods have at last lost their immemorial quietude." While exploring the Edward Thomas country in Hampshire, I noted: "Aircraft droning incessantly. During the past hour I doubt there's been five minutes of silence." While exploring the Hilaire Belloc country in Sussex, I noted: "Walked at Shipley for two hours, accompanied most of the time by aircraft." While exploring the Monmouthshire hills, I noted: "Even here the planes are rumbling."

Some regions, of course, long ago accustomed themselves to aircraft, but the din continues to increase and has infected many places that were formerly quiet. Thus, in April 1974 I described the Westmorland fells as "among the most peaceful places in England". But in April 1978 I noted: "Climbed Barbon Fell, aircraft buzzing like bad-tempered wasps." At Constable's mill near East Bergholt in Suffolk, I noted: "7.30 a.m. and a glorious May morning—everything spoiled by aircraft." While exploring the Norfolk coast at Blakeney, I noted: "These screeching rooftop aircraft remind me of the war." While exploring the Cornish coast at Gunwhalloe, I noted: "If only the aircraft would leave us. . ." While exploring the site of the Battle of Naseby in Northamptonshire, I noted: "Aircraft circling overhead. There seems no end to the monotonous whine." While seeking the stillness of Wordsworth's Alfoxden in Somerset, I noted: "The customary angry swarm is overhead." While making yet another visit to my former home in Buckinghamshire, I noted: "Though my roots here are ineradicable, I am thankful to have left . . . The old stillness is incessantly shattered by aircraft."

The latest victim of this modern malaise is a part of North Devon, where in 1976 I noted: "Except for occasional low-flying attacks, this outpost of Exmoor is as peaceful as any I know." In the same area, on 17th August 1978, I noted: "Twice wakened by low-flying aircraft between 11 p.m. and midnight. Then again at 4.03 a.m., 4.17, 4.36, 5.12, 6.22. Windows rattled each time. How on earth do the people manage to sleep?" Between breakfast and teatime next day, "the noise was like an approaching thunderstorm—bombers, fighters, helicopters, trainers. A rifle range at Filleigh kept up a barrage throughout the day, audible four miles away. Yet in

1976 the region seldom heard an aircraft". This din will soon become even worse because the North Devon Council and the North Devon MP, Jeremy Thorpe, have enthusiastically supported the re-opening of an RAF base only a few miles away. Opponents of the airfield tried in vain to point out the effects which the noise would have on tourism. In a letter to a local newspaper one hotelier remarked: "Visitors from industrial regions are willing to pay just in order to hear the blackbirds, but they certainly won't come here if the RAF bombards them day and night. Last week three of my own guests left after two days because of the low-level attacks."

When the history of the second half of the twentieth century comes to be written—assuming that any historian survives to write it, a latterday Cobbett or Massingham will cite the destruction of quietness, even in places where quietness seemed unassailable. Quietness itself is not, of course, the same as silence. Long before men arrived to deafen it, the Earth, like Prospero's isle, was full of "Sounds and sweet airs, that give delight, and hurt not". Wind and rain, sea and shingle, birdsong and sheep-bleat—all denoted movement, endeavour, life. When, therefore, a countryman speaks of quietness, he means an absence of the prolonged mechanical noise which drowns the music of streams, the voices of children, and an old man calling home the cows. If we are to enjoy the boons of technology (hygiene, leisure, the reduction of unskilled manual labour), we must endure also the banes of technology (noise, speed, the proliferation of tedious machine-minding). Lorries and cars now thunder along every main road and can be heard on many country lanes. One aircraft disturbs a million people in a few seconds. And if you enter a restaurant, hoping to blend good food with good talk, you will probably be greeted by a canned version of the cacophony which Robert Bridges detested:

a trifling music playeth, dispelling all thought
that while they fill the belly, the empty mind may float lightly on
                                                    the full
moonshine of o'er blown affluence.

A century ago, Gerard Manley Hopkins invoked the peace of the English countryside:

Elected silence, sing to me,
And beat upon my whorlèd ear,
Pipe me to pastures still, and be
The music that I care to hear.

But progress was already on the march, and when Hopkins
witnessed the destruction of beautiful trees near Oxford, he
mourned as much for posterity as for himself: "After-comers
cannot guess the beauty been . . ." Just so, some of us will
regret that our descendants may never enjoy those soothing
sounds which compose a country quietude. In the bad old days
man's inner voice whispered: "Be still, and know that I am
God." In the good new days man's inner voice shouts: "Be
noisy, and know that I am Progress."

9

A Clerical Dodo

There are moments in history when circumstances change so rapidly and so radically that they put an end to the propagation of a species or type of man. As a result, the type acquires in death a fame which in life it neither sought nor desired. Just such a fame will soon be thrust upon the Canon, who in his youth was by no means a rarity but is now something of a dodo.

This obsolescent cleric was born in 1899, second son of a squireen who had inherited an unexpected baronetcy and with it enough money to send his three boys to Oxford, at which place the Canon achieved an athletics Blue and a Double First. In 1916 he enlisted as a subaltern in his county yeomanry; in 1917 he won an MC; in 1918 he was wounded; in 1919 he went up to Oxford; and in 1926 he was ordained deacon. The next ten years were given to scholarship. Rumour, indeed, said that the scholar would succeed the Dean of his college, whereafter he might reasonably hope for another three decades of escalating eminence. Looking even further ahead, he sometimes thought that he would like to end his days as rector of the parish in which he had been born and of which his elder brother, a soldier was patron.

Then occurred one of those private events which sometimes alter a public career: the Canon married, and a year later his wife and son died in childbirth. The widower still believes that, on the morning of the funeral, God called him via the Post Office, which delivered a letter announcing the retirement of the rector of his native parish. So the bereaved scholar forsook the high road to preferment and went his way as a shepherd among the byelanes of a remote village. There was nothing histrionic in the self-rustication. The man who had captured a German battery was not likely to dive into the nearest funk-hole. Within a few months, therefore, he returned as rector of the church in which he had been baptized and confirmed and married. Thus it came about that a second Bemerton received another Herbert, a scholar, an aristocrat, a worldling who had wielded the sword. But the new rector's duties were not wholly strange to him, because he had spent several vacations as curate in an industrial town. Sagacity soon combined with courtesy to reach a compromise between his own Anglo-Catholicism and the broader outlook of the parishioners. From the very start, however, he exercised the prerogative of a benevolent master, so that on high feast days the altar blazed with candles, and the rector himself wore what his brother called "Reggie's regimentals".

The new incumbent had arrived at a time when the country parson was still *persona* or an important person in the parish. Most of the neighbouring clergy were graduates of Oxford or of Cambridge; all received a stipend greater than a machine-minder's; and none believed that Jesus was a homosexual Unitarian. Having assessed his flock, the rector summoned the organist from his old college, and together they decided how best to persuade anti-papal ploughmen to sing Gregorian plainsong. When the stoup in the porch was filled with holy water, the sexton tendered his resignation but withdrew it after the rector had asked him to read aloud the opening sentence of the Prayer Book: "It hath been the wisdom of the Church of England, ever since the first compiling of her Publick Liturgy, to hold the mean between the two extremes, of too much stiffness in refusing and of too much easiness in admitting any variation from it."

The rector made it known that his study was open to all comers between 2 p.m. and 3.30 p.m. every weekday except Wednesday, when he followed the beagles. He further announced that—even on beagling day—he himself was open to anyone in acute distress. The results were surprising, at least to some of the villagers, for whereas the work-shy trouble-maker went empty away, the girl with an illegitimate baby received a meal, a blessing, her fare home, and a letter to her parents. In those years, of course, a country parson enjoyed considerably more leisure than his successors do. He served as the shepherd of only one flock, not as the once-weekly chaplain to several. This happier state of affairs enabled the rector not only to burnish his scholarship but also to embellish it with learned papers, notably a re-examination of Vergil's Messianic eclogue.

So the slow years slipped by, mindful sometimes of a brilliant promise which had declined to fulfil itself, yet rejoicing always in the humbler and more rural harvest. During the 1940s, however, even the rector's sequestered parish felt the first cold wind of change. The neighbouring clergy either died or retired and were replaced by men whose piety was of a different kind. But the rector himself stood four-square against the storm. Like a more famous parson,

> Remote from towns he ran his godly race,
> Nor e'er had changed, nor wished to change, his place . . .

When his elder brother died without issue, the rector became 'the Rev. Sir Reginald', patron of his own living, both squire and parson. At Michaelmas he moved from the rectory to the manor house, where spiritual ministrations to his sheep were leavened with agricultural instructions to his shepherd. Some weeks later he took his seat in a Canon's stall, feeling downcast when the Lessons were read in Welfare English, and utterly dejected when the sermon pleaded for "a deeper understanding of all that is best in Marxism". Dejection turned to disgust when a local parson wished to celebrate Mass with the aid of a Pop Group whose members had recently spent six months as non-paying guests in one of Her Majesty's more austere public institutions. Like his close friend Dean Inge, the Canon trod eclectically among orthodox dogma. To a Regius Professor of Divinity, with whom he had been discussing the Thirty-Nine Articles, he confessed: "In my less exalted moments I sometimes feel that there are at least thirty-eight too many of them." Yet in his heart of hearts, and always from the pulpit, he could with a good conscience surmount the Pauline stumbling blocks. "That man," he once said, "has no right to be a bishop. He has no right to be a deacon. In fact, he hasn't even the right to call himself a Christian.''

Assisted nowadays by a younger cleric, the old scholar still offers Canon's opinion on many topics, from Greek epigraphy and village fêtes to Roman mythology and Erastian archdeacons. Although his own world has almost disappeared, the new generation continues to need his knowledge of human nature and of the great thoughts and deeds which men have achieved down the centuries.

Harvest Home

In summer our great expectations are seldom fulfilled. In autumn our modest hopes are rarely rebuffed. Everyone remembers snow in May, frost in June, floods in July, droughts in August; but of September—as of childhood—we remember chiefly the good things, not least because for most of us they outnumber the bad. Today, for example, the flowers are vivid as they were in June. Like the time-honoured tenants of a country garden, they never fall into arrears—marigolds, sweetwilliams, roses, antirrhinums, asters, petunias, pansies, dahlias, chrysanthemums, honeysuckle, foxgloves—all those old familiar faces have achieved a kind of renascence after August's heat, and now they bask in an air so calm that last night's bonfire still glows near the waste heap, as in Ruth Pitter's rural scene:

> Up sweetly on the autumn air
> Spiced funeral vapours rise.

The brilliance of a summer dawn often ends in cloud, whereas September often disperses an early mist. This morning the sky remained overcast until the sun broke through at eleven o'clock, foretelling a warm afternoon. Only one cloud was visible, a small white disc with serrated edges. There being no wind, the shipless sail seemed to be anchored on a limitless Aegean. You looked up at it, then turned away and then again looked up and turned away, and still the sail had not moved more than an inch beyond the middle of the hilltop tree. If you climbed the meadow, looking for mushrooms, you soon felt hot.

From the wood adjoining this garden I can hear no sound at all until a bee bumbles by, whereafter the stillness returns until a rook flaps overhead, uttering sounds as harsh as the place-name which Beethoven likened to the squeaking of a rusty axle, *Gneizendorf*. Hearing it, two robins send a challenge, followed by a blackbird's metallic alarm call. Then once more the

stillness returns, heightened by the presence of a combine harvester that waits like a dumb juggernaut whose blades mime a scarlet windmill against a blue sky. The machine reeks of oil and is warm to touch. Surrounded by such silence, one might almost suppose that the land had hibernated and that those who tilled it were likewise taking a long siesta. Even the cows have stopped grazing and are either flicking their tails against the flies or kneeling as if in worship of the sun. But all this noonday idleness is deceptive because the land has, in fact, reached the zenith of its annual achievement. Day after day, near and far, the harvest tractors hum tirelessly. In the Cambridgeshire Fens and on Salisbury Plain, where some of the fields are so vast that you cannot see the hedgerows dividing them, the combines crawl like crabs across endless golden sands. On these Exmoor hills, however, the working horse has not yet become redundant. One of our farmers still cuts the corn as his grandfather cut it, with a horse-hauled reaper. He has also stooked the corn in sheaves that stand like amber statues, each broad-based column climbing gracefully to a fruitful apex. A moment ago, when a breeze stirred, I could just hear the creak of wagons, the thud of hooves, and a faint "Whoa, my 'ansome!"

In August and September the harvesters are afield early, eager to exploit the light and warmth. Sometimes they work late by moonshine, cutting or carting. Deprived of their drink at the inn, they welcome the beer and cider which the farmer's wife delivers in a wagon returning from the barn. They drink deep and slow. "That's better, missus. Reckon us be 'alfway to coming alive again." Summer or autumn, it is all one to the men and women who give us our daily bread. They have neither the time nor the inclination to admire a pretty view. If their thoughts ever do stray from the present task, it is solely in order to anticipate the next, the ploughing, and after that the sowing and after that the reaping and after that sowing and after that the same cyclic skills which, like a physician's, are a blend of science and intuition, for it is useless to ask a farmer to define the logic which tells him that his corn is ripe. He cannot answer your question because he does not know the answer. If he does reply, he will probably say: "It's partly the look of the crop." But when you ask him to define the look, again he will shake his head, saying: "It's something you learn. I'll tell you this, though . . . you don't learn it in a day, nor in a year neither." When you remark that the grain must be rubbed, to test its hardness, the farmer will agree; but again he will fail to define the hardness. Rubbing a thumb and forefinger together, he will mutter: "It's something else you learn. Corn's not like water, you know. You can't take its temperature."

Technology is even now planning to build a Britain whose fields are tilled and sown and reaped with machines, driven by one man at a remote-control panel. The small farm will disappear, swallowed by enormous estates, most of them owned by non-resident industrialists and financiers and ultimately by a Civil Service whose sole concern is to increase productivity at all costs—even at the cost of the land's ability to produce. The majority of farmhands will become machine-minders, scarcely distinguishable from the urban masses who spray cars, wrap cigarette cartons, and obey only the shop steward who obeys *them*. Pray hard, that you may die before the nightmare comes true.

Fortunately, Exmoor itself will never become an outdoor factory. Its hills are too high, and many of its acres too rugged, for the kind of "intensive" farming that interests deskbound financiers and State-controlling planners. Untroubled therefor by noise and fumes, the one fleecy cloud still loiters, as though reluctant to approach the sun lest it suffer the fate of Icarus. Such bountiful quietude evokes Gerald Bullett's empathy with the season of mellow fruitfulness:

> So rare the fallen fleece of sky,
> So far the noise of men,
> Myself for a musing moment
> Was blackbird, was wren.

The Man with the Moneybags

On Saturday mornings he stands tweedily plus-foured beside a field-gate, serving as honorary secretary of the beagles, tactfully detecting any follower who has forgotten, or for some other reason failed, to pay the price of a day's hunting. Being still in his forties, he can keep up with the field, but the field knows that he sometimes chooses not to keep up, as, for example, when he halts to quiz a new combine harvester or to assess a field of kale. A similar inquisitiveness may be seen in his behaviour as honorary treasurer of the cricket club, for while the rest of the spectators are applauding a six, or bewailing a duck, he himself is noting the old farmer's new car and the new stockbroker's old boots. All this, of course, he does discreetly, rather as a doctor observes the florid complexion and the tremulous hand. On Saturday, then, he is an open air man; but on Monday he sits in the local bank, behind a door marked 'Manager'.

At his first post, as junior cashier in a London suburb, he knew as little about corn as about coal; later, however, his transference to South Wales enabled him to acquire a useful knowledge of the steel industry, together with information about poultry and pigs, gleaned from several smallholding customers. Soon after his thirtieth birthday, he spent some weeks as locum at a fishing village, whence he returned with a taste for sailing and a knowledge of the herring trade. Today, as manager in a small country town, he draws on those varied experiences: witness his trustful overdraft to the seedsman, and his wary wait-and-see to the spinster who did not know that a strike-bound factory is one of the reasons why people hesitate to invest in British industry.

Like the priest and the doctor, a bank manager is often surprised by the nature of the secrets which he must keep. Only last week our beagling manager took tea at a cottage where the curtains were moth-eaten, the windowpanes were cracked, and a rusty oil stove glimmered in the fireless hearth; yet the manager knew that his host could lawfully write a cheque for £10,000. Next day the manager interviewed a customer whose Rolls-Royce concealed from the public—though not from the bank—that Amalgamated Loans Ltd lived by borrowing from Peter in order to survive long enough to repay Paul.

The status of a bank manager has soared with the cost of living. Elderly villagers can recall the years when a bank employee entered the manor house via the side door, and was not eligible for membership of the Hunt committee. Today the manager mingles with doctors and lawyers, and may on occasion summon the squire into his presence ("I suggest you postpone the new swimming-pool until we've settled that little matter of three thousand"). On certain kinds of committee the manager is almost *sine qua non*. If he happens to be a churchgoer, he will probably become keeper of the parish purse, a task that may require him to suggest, though never to betray, a professional secret. Thus, while helping to decide who shall receive the Michaelmas gift of a goose, he shakes his head when the rector murmurs: "Poor young Perkis, do you think?" Unlike the priest, the banker knows that for the past eighteen months poor young Perkis has been drawing so much National Assistance, and doing so many tax-free odd jobs, that he now owns a colour-television set. The banker, however, is by no means a Scrooge, for although he never allows compassion to confound commerce, he has more than once granted a chanceful loan, rather like Crabbe's rural trustee: "To give in secret was a favourite act."

The beaglers, at all events, regard their honorary secretary as a thoroughly good sport. They admire especially the expertise with which he transferred a surplus of £12 from Consols to International Mines, as a result of which the unpaid whips received £5 apiece toward the cost of new breeches. Moreover, his skill at legally balancing a farmer's budget has led several other followers to invite him to achieve a comparable deficit on their own account.

Village banks were rare during the early years of the twentieth century, when people considered themselves fortunate if they received once-weekly visits from a cashier who conducted business at a customer's shop (in some villages this still occurs). Not a few Edwardian farmhands entrusted their savings to a Friendly Society while others stuffed the money into crevices which burglars often discovered. Small shopkeepers were not above hiding their cash in a stocking under a floorboard (and that, too, still occurs). Even today some of the older farmfolk merely sign their cheques, leaving the payee to add the date, the name, and the amount of money. There was something to be said both for and against the old private banks, each issuing its own promissory notes, all competing to the customers' advantage, and none immune against insolvency. Several of the country banks were founded by businessmen as subsidiaries to their other local ventures. Such a one was started at Wisbech by James Hill, grandfather of Octavia Hill, a co-founder of the National Trust. When the bank failed in 1835, Hill managed to pay his creditors and ultimately to re-open the bank. In 1840, however, more than one hundred banks were ruined, and this time Hill did not recover. Some of the bankrupt bankers paid part of their debts in kind, using corn, machinery, timber, and other commodities from their factories and warehouses. Such were the men of whom foreigners said: "An Englishman's word is his bond."

Our own beagling banker looks back wistfully to the time when his grandfather cycled from sub-branch to sub-branch, carrying hundreds of pounds in cash, having publicly announced that he would reach such-and-such a place at such-and-such a time. Not once in thirty years was he ever molested by a victim of social deprivation. His grandson, on the other hand, cashes-and-carries via Armour-Plated Cars Ltd, and thinks twice before sending one of his girls across the street with a pounds worth of coppers.

Reading between the Lines

From the quietness of his Buckinghamshire garden William Cowper uttered a *cri-de-cœur*:

> My soul is sick, with every day's report
> Of wrong and outrage with which the Earth is filled.

Since Cowper lived before railways arrived and before radio was imagined, his seclusion at Olney was in many ways deeper than any which now exists on this planet. When he did receive a newspaper, it was probably several days old, containing foreign despatches that may have been several weeks old when they reached the printer. How much more insistent is the bad news which hourly assails everyone who reads or hears the latest bulletin. As Dr Johnson remarked, news consists either of disaster averted or of disaster incurred. Nevertheless, to blame journalists for spreading gloom is thrice unjust: first, because sadness and disaster are not created by journalists; second, because sadness and disaster must in some degree be shared by all who care for humanity; third, because sadness and disaster exert a macabre fascination. To those three facts may be added a fourth, namely that a newspaper which suppressed every item of bad news would soon go bankrupt. One is reminded of Thomas de Quincey, who served for a while as editor of the *Westmorland Gazette*, a paper which still informs and entertains the inhabitants of that ancient county. Instead of announcing a British victory at sea, or the price of pigs at Penrith, de Quincey preferred to publish news about local antiquities. One can almost hear the farmers turning the pages in vain: "Dammit, theer's nowt a word o'what heifers are fetching in Kendal." Despite his architectural prose, de Quincey was soon relieved of his post.

Now the fact that the amount of sin per head of the population is greater in a city than in a village cannot be explained away in terms of social deprivation and other material dialectics, because the wages and so-called amenities in a city are as a rule better than the wages and so-called amenities in a village. If a lack of money really were the root of all evil, then every millionaire would wear a halo, and all poets would be in prison. However, when the news is especially bad, even the most equable countryman begins to wonder whether decency and goodness do still exist on Earth. A moment's reflection—or, better still, an hour's walk—will correct his doleful perspective, starting at the crossroads, where the walker is greeted by a young couple strolling arm-linked through an Eden that has never heard of strikes and wars and economic crises.

At the next crossroads the walker is overtaken by a woman motorist who says: "Can I give you a lift? Or are you just out for a walk?" Recognizing the motorist, the walker remembers that Mrs A is making her weekly visit to Miss B who is bedridden, and dearly loves a chat. Further uplane, the walker notices a farmer tending a cow. "'Tis nobbut a scratch," the man explains, "but I'd not like t'owd gal to suffer." From the summit of the next hill the walker sees a cottage whose eldest son was lately in trouble with the police. That the lad has now mended his waywardness is due chiefly to a social worker who spent several months patiently proving that sternness and compassion are often more efficacious than sloppiness and a warning.

Approaching a village, the walker hears the happy hubbub of a school whose teacher has for the past decade nursed her mother, though she might easily have sent the invalid to a hospital. Year after year, unsung and uncomplaining, the teacher spends her life serving the very old and the rather young. Although she may regret that her salary is much smaller than that of a goalkeeper or a prize-fighter, she does not go on strike. Being old-fashioned, she does what she is paid to do, even although the payment may seem inadequate.

From the summit of yet another hill the walker can just glimpse the roofs of a market town; and there, also, the people are getting on with the job, taking the rough with the smooth, unobtrusively performing those little acts of kindness which Wordsworth rated as "the best portion of a good man's life". Since the walker often visits that town, he knows about its acts of kindness—the teenager who helps the Old Folks' Club, the vicar who donates anonymously from a meagre stipend, the housewife who offers a home to battered babies, the arthritic cripple who is more cheerful than the hale dustman, the worker who refuses to join a union whose aims he distrusts and whose methods he despises.

Some people will protest that the walker had merely wasted an hour by indulging sentimental platitudes. But the protest does not disturb him. To the charge of sentimentality or excessive emotion he replies: "What's excessive about bandaging a wound, or nursing a relative, or defying a tyrant?" By the time he reaches his home, the walker has read between the headlines, seeing therein those items which few of us regard as news. He has learned, for example, that the people whom he met during his walk are like millions of other people throughout the world—frail, fallible, vulnerable to any scribbler who chooses to grow rich by mocking them, yet are the salt and the sugar of this earth. Delve as deeply as you please into the murk of human motive, still you are left with the fact that some people are more likely to light a candle than to curse the darkness. King Lear's eldest daughter summed it up when she cried: "O, the difference of man and man!" And Robert Louis Stevenson summed it up, too, when he said: "The average man is a truly courageous person and truly fond of living."

Life, then, goes on, but the headlines die next day. We have weathered worse times than these, and have survived to enjoy better. Despite his pessimism, Thomas Hardy believed that neither wars nor rumours of wars shall ever eclipse the young couple whom our walker met in the lane:

Yonder a maid and her wight
Come whispering by:
War's annals will cloud into night
Ere their story die.

10

Springtime in Autumn

During the memorable drought of 1976 a large area of the kingdom was parched, and hundreds of thousands of people did what Ruth was told to do: "When thou art athirst, go unto the vessels and drink of that which the young men have drawn." But in Britain's brown and thirsty land it was not only the young men who drew water from a stand-pipe; old women went there, clutching a plastic bucket.

Civil engineering is not among my accomplishments, but I do know that countless villagers annually run short of water when townsfolk flock to the coast and country. Fortunately, I possess my own supply, which comes from a spring, thirty-five feet below the ground, flowing past the bottom of a shaft that was dug by the miners who once worked on what is now my land. Needless to say, they built the shaft handsomely and efficiently, so that it resembles a stone-walled tunnel, wide enough for a man to climb up and down in comfort, or at any rate without grazing his elbows. When I first came to live here, a hygienic friend expressed horror that I had omitted to analyse the spring. He cited the fatal diseases which come of drinking foul water. He predicted my early demise. Indeed, he could scarcely believe that it had not already occurred. I replied that the house had been drawing water from the spring for at least three hundred years and that many of the householders had lived to a great age (the previous occupant died suddenly, while sitting in the sun, not far short of his eighty-fifth birthday). None of this could reassure my friend, for whenever we meet, he is evidently amazed to find me still alive.

Of the quality of the spring water I am not competent to speak, but of its taste I know a good deal, having drunk it for a considerable number of years; and my knowledge was confirmed by two incidents. The first occurred while some workmen, who were making structural alterations to the house, persistently observed the go-slow maxim of the author of *Lorna Doone*: "No Devonshire man ever thinks of working harder than his Maker meant for him." In an attempt to speed the workmen's progress, I took to issuing a ration of beer at noon. On the fourth day, noticing that the beer was unopened, I inquired the reason. "We've just had a drink from your spring," the foreman replied. "It's the best water we ever tasted." Coming from confirmed alcophiles, that was indeed a compliment, all the more appreciated because I am—as Wordsworth said of himself—"A simple water-drinking Bard". Admittedly, I will sometimes take a sociable glass of sherry, to show that my temperance is gourmand rather than moral; but the noises which issue from a public house at closing time persuade me that *in aqua sanitas* is a better condition than *in vino inanitatis*.

The second of the two incidents occurred during a thirsty walk, when I called at a farmhouse to beg a cup of water. The stuff came from the mains, and only an old-fashioned courtesy prevented me from spitting it into the sink. On arriving home, I rinsed away the taste by drinking some of my own spring water. Unfortunately, the spring is not a hardy perennial. At any time between the end of June and the beginning of August the water level falls below the pump's power to raise it. I therefore installed a reservoir in one of the paddocks, which is filled from the spring in March and thereafter replenished with rainwater from the roof. By such means I am able to remain slaked and bathed until the autumnal rains cause the springs to break. Sometimes they break so gently that their renascence can be gauged only by watching the level of the streams: at other times (especially after prolonged rainfall) they break so gushingly that the sound of their music gladdens the heart that has been sickened by the sight of withered grass, cast-iron earth, dusty lanes, and listless leaves. This morning, for instance, all the hills exude miniature replicas of that precipitous Yorkshire Niagara which seethes down the rock-face of a fell near Sedbergh, aptly named Cautley Spout. Here on Exmoor the North Devon lanes are flanked by helter-skelter rivulets that carry all, or very nearly all, before them—twigs, leaves, fleece, straws, pebbles, grass, and any other flotsam and jetsam that have been co-opted willy-nilly as a cascading cargo. On every lane the torrents are as ingenious as a sheep seeking a way out, for although their impetus will ultimately create a barrier, they always contrive either to undermine or to overflow it, so that an accumulation of debris, two feet tall and apparently impregnable, suddenly collapses and is swept downhill to repeat the process. Drains are as loud as mouths that have over-stuffed themselves; and if any object is too large to pass through the grid, it lies there quivering, metronomically lifted and dropped by the spate beneath it. On the steepest lanes the tide is truly impressive, and if you walk against them, the waves splash your knees. One of the twigs floats upright like a mast; another carries with it a yard of couch grass; a third, having almost broken its back, twirls round and round like the hand of a haywire clock. Once or twice you notice a dead mouse, or the skull of a rabbit, or a fragment of sheep's jawbone. Sometimes a bus ticket scurries past, pursued by a cardboard carton and a cork-tipped fag-end. I have actually seen a yard of corrugated metal slithering downhill at a brisk four knots. The poet was justified when he exclaimed:

> The springs have broken: all the lanes
> Gurgle above the glutted drains
> Where dribs and drabs of fallen leaves
> That sailed away from autumn eaves
> Now pile themselves in sodden sheaves
> While every brooklet surges
> In spate beside the verges.

Although it sings an introit for autumnal gales, this breaking of the springs is a welcome event, symbolizing both a promise and the fulfilment thereof, at whose behest the grass recovers its greenness, the flowers are slaked, the land is rinsed, and the roots add an imperceptible cubit to their stature.

Signs of the Times

I may claim to possess a knowledge of country inns that would do credit to the most tippling of itinerant topers. This knowledge will seem strange in an almost total abstainer who seldom drinks unless he feels thirsty. On my own pub crawls I usually ask for coffee, and if that is unavailable, I purchase either a glass of tomato juice or a box of matches, thus buying time in which to sample the smoke-stained rafters, the country talk, and the sign above the door.

Nobody knows when the first inn sign was erected, nor what it depicted. Our present signs are probably descended from the various tokens with which the mediæval ale-wives drew attention to their wares. Since then, of course, the tokens have multiplied. Even without consulting my notebooks I can cite 'The Squinting Cat', 'Who'd Have Thought It', 'Trouble-House', 'Printer's Devil', 'Cardinal's Error', 'Hole in the Wall', 'Case is Altered', 'Pindar of Wakefield', 'Driftwood Spars', 'Air Balloon'. Some of the names are corruptions of a meaningful original, such as 'St Peter ad Vincula' (which became 'St Peter's Finger') and 'The Hospice' (which became 'The Ostrich').

Inn signs may offer a clue not only to the date of a foundation but also to its re-naming. Thus, the Charlie Butler Inn at Wandsworth commemorates the man who in 1976 completed forty-two years' service as groom to the Shire horses that delivered the beer. Likewise when Nelson received command of HMS *Agamemnon* in 1743, he gave a dinner for the villagers at Burnham Thorpe, his Norfolk birthplace, where the inn now bears his name (and the adjacent shop is called Trafalgar Stores). Other famous men speak for themselves via 'The Wellington', 'The Sherlock Holmes', 'The Winston Churchill' and 'The Tumbledown Dick', alias His Highness the Lord Protector Richard Cromwell, ineffectual son and heir of Oliver, England's military dictator.

Beware of being misled by inns that call themselves new, for some of them are very old. The New Inn at Gloucester, for example, was built to accommodate pilgrims to the shrine of

King Edward II, who had been murdered at Berkeley Castle. The New Inn at Gawcot in Buckinghamshire was already old when Edward Gibbon passed—and may have patronized it—on the way to his neighbouring manor at Lenborough. I know of one inn which prides itself on having a frame for the sign, but no sign in the frame. This is 'The Lonely White Horse', hiding at the end of a track among the hills above Petersfield in Hampshire. When Edward Thomas visited the inn, shortly before 1914, he was told that someone had stolen the sign and then chucked it into a pond; a fact which he mentioned in his poem *Up in the Wind*:

> it took a thief
> To move it, and we've never had another.
> It's lying at the bottom of the pond.

Very rare are the inns bearing the names of two people. I recall 'The Pink and Lily', not far from my former home overlooking Bledlow Ridge in the Chilterns, whose name is matrimonial rather than horticultural, a Pink having married a Lily, whereafter the couple set up as publicans. Rupert Brooke used to stay at this place. Indeed, he presented his host with a manuscript poem. I remember, too, the inn that was once the home of Adam and his wife Eve in a place called Paradise. They had thought of calling the inn 'Paradise Regained', but eventually they chose 'Adam and Eve'.

Concerning England's highest inn there is some dispute but no doubt. Cheshiremen have long maintained that the honour belongs to 'The Cat and Fiddle', which stands sixteen hundred feet among the mists of Macclesfield Forest; but the rightful claimant is Tan Hill Inn, which faces the Pennine Way, far from a village, along the border between Westmorland and Yorkshire. Built during the eighteenth century, the place was originally called 'King's Pit House', a reference to the adjacent coal workings. When I first visited Tan Hill Inn, many years ago, a handwritten note on the door stated 'Closed for Decorations' (it happened to be one of the few occasions when I really did feel thirsty). However, a builder's ladder leaned against the wall, so I climbed it in order to take a photograph of a plaque over the entrance, which said that the inn was the highest in England, more than seventeen hundred feet above sea level. Many mediæval and Tudor taverns carried sacred names: 'The Angel', 'Lamb and Flag', 'Noah's Ark', 'Cross Keys', 'Mitre', 'Seven Stars', 'Ring o'Bells', 'Church House', 'Trip to Jerusalem'. One or two inns canonized themselves as 'St George', or 'St Blaise', or 'St Catherine'. So far as I know, however, only one inn was ever built by a clergyman. It stands at the head of Kirkstone Pass in Westmorland, and was intended to serve as a hospice for snowbound travellers.

During my childhood in north Buckinghamshire I used often to wonder what The Steamboat Inn was doing, so far from the sea. Other people wondered, too, and whenever they inquired of the landlord, he would point to the canal outside the door, saying: "In the old days a paddleboat passed this pub. All smoke and sparks she was. Good for trade, though 'cause there ain't nothing loike sparks and smoke for making a marn warnt to whet 'is whistle. Oi've 'eard say as some of 'em came in 'ere thart thirsty they'd ha' drunk a glass o' water even."

Several inns have been inscribed by poets, of whom the doyen was Burns, among whose accomplishments Robert Bridges listed "drinking and kissing". Burns certainly pencilled a poem on the chimney-piece of the inn at Kenmore ("These northern scenes with weary feet I tread"); and on a window of 'The King's Arms' at Dumfriess he scratched a praise of the excisemen who collected the tax on liquor. Such praise would not have pleased W. H. Davies, a lifelong non-water-drinker, who told John Masefield, who ultimately told me, that he, Davies, was sitting in The Coach and Horses when he composed the following *cri-de-cœur*:

> They're taxing Ale again, I hear,
> A penny more the can;
> They're taxing poor old Ale again,
> The only honest man.

A Nip in the Air

Someone somewhere sometime in October says: "There's quite a nip in the air." The date and place of that ancient utterance will vary, because the British climate is a notorious flouter of calendars. The first week in October can be milder than the last week in May; the last week in October can be colder than the first week in January; and while Kent suffers a week of grey skies, Caithness may collect seven sunny days.

During your own daily walk you may observe the various responses to October's cold shoulder. Thus, in a shed behind his forge the farrier is sawing a tree which he felled last winter; this evening the logs will crackle fragrantly on the hearth. Passing the Hall, you notice that last night's frost has littered the drive with a mosaic of brown and yellow leaves and a few green hollies, victims of a gale that preceded the lull before the frost. Everything seems very still, for although the blackbirds and thrushes do sometimes sing in autumn, theirs is an attenuated tune, brief and half-hearted. The only sustained song is the robin's, which sounds especially melodious above the pervasive silence. Some people find the song so enjoyable that they halt awhile in order to hear it. Rooks, of course, are hoarse and hardy perennials, and at sundown you can hear them a mile away.

Just beyond the church you pass a group of roadmen shovelling grit from a lorry. "At six o'clock this morning," they tell you, "this lane was like a skating rink. They say old Grannie Newton went shopping on 'er backside. Ah, and they say 'twill freeze again tonight. Let's 'ope we don't get no snow. I reckon December's quite soon enough for that sort o'caper."

Having reached the Manse, you meet the minister's sister, who says: "Is it me, or does everyone else feel cold?"

Near the crossroads, where a gate leads into a field, the grass three days ago was hidden under so much mud that even to tiptoe across it was to splash your knees; but this morning the ruts are frozen stiff, and the puddles glower like grey seas on dark days. In the field itself the rabbits let go little salvos while they lope through the stubble. Halfway across the field you smell and presently see a bonfire, the work of an old man who is trimming the hedge. Nearby, his dog sits patiently under a haversack slung from an upright spade. You pause to exchange platitudes.

"Quite a fresh wind this morning."

"Too true," the hedger nods.

"Good for the gardens, though."

"True again. There's nothing like a frost for breaking down the clods." He stoops to crumble a fistful of earth. "This yere's as good as gold. In fact, 'tis better 'cause you can't turn gold into food."

"But you can use it to buy food from other nations."

"Only if other nations buy your hardware. And according to the newspapers they'm making their own nowadays. Either that or buying it from countries where they don't go on strike every 'arf-our." He shakes his head. "It seems downright crazy to me, all these factories and not enough food to feed 'em for a fortnight."

"That's the way it is," you reply.

The hedger then expresses a doubt by asking a question: "Do you reckon there's any future in farming?"

"If there isn't, there's no future for anyone. As you say, we can't cook gold, and we certainly can't eat invisible exports."

"Ah, well." He whets the bill-hook. "Future or not, I've still another dozen yards before dinnertime."

"You make a better job of it than the machines do."

"So I should 'ope. Some of those contraptions are worse than a barber who's never seen a pair of scissors." He surveys his handiwork, each branch bent and snicked just so, then interlaced and again trimmed. "If you want a good suit of clothes, you get 'em made by hand. If you want a portrait of yourself, you get that made by hand, too. And if you want your appendicitis took out, you don't go to a machine for it." He stares at his own work-worn hand. "I reckon th' Almighty did a good job when he made this 'en."

"They say the hand evolved itself."

"So I've 'eard. But who taught it to evolve?" He takes a swig of tea from the flask in his haversack. "We'd a professor down yere last summer, telling us that the world 'appened by chance. I said to my missus afterwards, 'If 'ee's what they call a clever fellow,' I said, 'then thank God I was born a bloody fool.'" He replaces the flask in the haversack. "I couldn't 'elp but laugh, though, 'cause the very next day the professor said 'ee'd just solved a difficult problem. 'That's a bit o'luck,' I told 'en. 'Luck?' he said. 'It wasn't luck.' 'Begging your pardon,' I reminded 'im, 'but last night you told us that everything 'appened by chance.'"

Now the old man makes a nonchalant sweep with the blade. "Looks easy, eh?"

"It always is easy, when you know how."

"The first time I ever tried, with my old Dad looking on, I'd to keep bending down to see if I'd cut deep enough. But now," he makes a second sweep, "'tis as though the hand and the brain are reciting something they'd learned by heart without needing to look at the words." He slips a length of twine round a cluster of twigs. "I suppose 'tis only a little thing when you compare it with building a bridge or writing a book. Still, 'tis my job, or one of 'em. I've mastered it, I've come to like it, and I've been doing it near sixty years. How many other people nowadays can say that about their own job?"

Suddenly he gives a slight shiver. "This won't do, standing

around gossiping." He bends a branch with his left hand. "You've to keep moving when there's a nip in the air."

The Heart of Rural Britain

Edward Thomas once travelled in a train that was briefly halted by a signal at Adlestrop in the Cotswolds. Although the other passengers may have resented the unscheduled opportunity to observe and meditate, Thomas himself enjoyed a summer interlude that enabled him to admire the scene while

> a blackbird sang
> Close by, and round him, mistier,
> Farther and farther, all the birds
> of Oxfordshire and Gloucestershire.

Some critics have rebuked Thomas for ignoring the social problems of rural life. Instead of babbling about blackbirds, he ought to have protested against low wages, insanitary cottages, and all the other harsh facts of life during the early years of the twentieth century. But countless people can, and too often do, write political pamphlets, whereas very few people indeed can write good poetry. In any event, Thomas was not a pamphleteer. His themes transcend and at the same time subsume current affairs. Moreover, Thomas himself had no reason to suppose that within a relatively short time the old order would be swept away, for rural England during the reign of Edward VII bore many resemblances to rural England during the reign of George IV. Tractors, for example, were unknown. Radio and television and motorways were unknown. Most of the great estates were still intact. Most of the cottagers worked either on the land or as ancillaries to those who did so work, and few of them travelled far beyond their market town. In 1914 no one could have foreseen the social and mechanical changes that were soon to transform so large a part of rural life. Yet most of us continue to hanker after a countryside that has died and will never revive. Sickened by industrial life, we long to escape from the fumes and noise, forgetful that by escaping we destroy the thing we seek, because quietness is incompatible with an overflow of refugees. Nevertheless, we still like to see a thatched cottage and a Shire horse; and when the hotelier apologizes because the television is out of action, we feel that we have indeed entered into the simple life.

There seems no end to our self-deception, our blend of wishful thinking and plain ignorance. Gazing down on a village in the valley, we notice the Norman church, the Tudor manor house, the Georgian tavern, the Victorian railway station. "This," we exclaim, "is England as it used to be." And some of us believe our own nonsense. We either do not know or will not admit that the heart of rural Britain has changed its tempo. The Norman church is one of five others served by a non-resident rector. The owners of the manor house were taxed out of it forty years ago, and the place is now a research centre for Synthetic Products Ltd. The tavern teems with weekend strangers who have motored twenty-five miles in order to sample the roast duckling. The railway station was closed in 1960, and its waiting-room has been wrecked by the reluctant recipients of compulsory education.

In 1900 nearly all the working villagers were employed by one or other of the neighbouring estates, as farmhands, foresters, carpenters, masons, gardeners, gamekeepers, domestic servants, coachmen, grooms. The Home Farm, which formerly employed ten men and six horses, now makes do with three lads and a couple of tractors. The blacksmith's forge is Betty's Boutique, the wheelwright's shop is Radio Renters, the Dissenting chapel is an artist's studio, the primary school is a factory, the parsonage belongs to an absentee stockbroker, and Paradise Lane will soon be 'developed' as an 'access approach' to a motorway whose distant rumble is heard throughout the day and night. A beauty spot on the edge of the village, first publicized by the tourist trade in 1966, attracts thousands of summer migrants whose vehicles block the street. Visitors at the tavern pay more for a ploughman's lunch than the ploughman's father earned in several days' hard labour; and newcomers from an industrial zone have ensured that moonlight and starlight are now dimmed by the glare of an artificial constellation. The true villagers—the men and women who were born there and have worked there and wish to die there—these are a dwindling minority. Innovation has made them feel as though they were strangers in their own countryside.

But, you may protest, there are still some villages that have achieved a happier balance between the new ways and the old. That is true, yet neither in the Grampians nor among the solitudes of Dartmoor are the old ways more than skin deep. How could it be otherwise? Women who in their youth walked to market with £1 to feed three mouths for seven days, now watch their granddaughter drive twenty miles to a town wherein £1 does not cover the cost of the journey. Is this a better state of affairs, or a worse? It is both. Few people would willingly return to country life in 1900 or even in 1930, when pneumonia was a killer, and water closets were a luxury. Whether our craving for security and comfort is wholly a good thing may be debated. It is certainly the chief reason why so few of us are able to live far from the screech of traffic, the roar of aircraft, and the scurry of commerce.

So, let us agree that the travel brochures and their thatched cottages are mere tellers of fairy tales. Let us admit that the Norman church is nine-tenths empty, that the plough team has gone the way of all flesh and that the majority of countryfolk no longer work on the land. Such honesty will save us from feeling disappointed when we discover that the village green is a car park and that many of the villagers would gladly exchange their Tudor cottage for a nice new bungalow near the lovely new super-mart.

Odd-Man-Out

One suspects that every generation has mourned the passing of "the last of the great eccentrics". Even David may have said to Goliath: "You'll never be the man your father was."

Myself, I like to think that I can recognize and applaud the ways in which science has heightened the pleasures by lowering the pains of existence. I certainly would not wish to suffer the dangers and discomforts of country life a century ago, and I doubt that many children would long survive a repetition of the perils of infant mortality three centuries ago, when a mother felt thankful if four of her seven offspring lived to celebrate their twenty-first birthday. I hope, therefore, that no one will accuse me of under-rating the present if I remark that the number of our eccentrics has decreased and seems likely to go on decreasing. Eccentricity is, of course, a matter of temperament. Genes not only engender eccentricity but also mould our definition of it. The word itself comes from the Greek *ekkentros*, meaning *a circle that is not concentric with other circles.* Modern geometricians would prefer to speak of "a square peg in a round hole".

Most people always have tended to conform with a norm. In Communist countries the conformity is compulsory. In capitalist countries it is induced more subtly by means of advertising, education, and other forms of brain-washing. Freudians may insist that the old-fashioned upbringing of children was bound to produce many pathological adults. My own definition of eccentricity excludes those symptoms of mild neurosis and advancing years which are rather the rule than an exception to it.

If I go the rounds of any half-dozen parishes which I know well, I find great difficulty in naming more than a couple of true eccentrics. If, on the other hand, I glance back at my childhood, I discover a galaxy of them, starting with Ebenezer, or 'Old Eb', who worked a horse-hauled barge along the canal and contrived to keep a 'wife' and a child in three ports-of-call. None of the women lived above twenty miles from the other two, and all remained unaware of the others' existence. If you protest that Old Eb's eclectic paternalism was a true norm and that monogamy is an aberration from it, still you must allow that Eb furthered his claim to eccentricity by attending a Roman Catholic church on the first Sunday in each month, an Anglican church on the second Sunday, a Baptist chapel on the third Sunday, and a public house on the fourth. My grandfather, a parson, used to say that Eb was hedging his bets in an attempt to ensure his own salvation.

I remember also Mrs Munday, a village shopkeeper, who closed early on her name-day. Then there was Mr Brown (he insisted on the Mr) who lived and slept in the same room as his pony. When the health inspectors did at last arrive, Mr Brown assured them: "Thart animal's proper 'ousetrained. And anyow oi always lets 'im out when 'ee seems to warnt to."

In 1930 I met a gamekeeper who invariably wore the costume of an Edwardian sportsman—to wit, Norfolk jacket, knickerbockers, gaiters and deer-stalker hat. The costume might have seemed less eccentric were it not for the fact that the game-keeper's small son was dressed as a replica of his father. The pair were known locally as Great and Little Titch, names that will arouse memories among venerable theatre-goers.

In 1940 I met a country parson who sometimes walked the lanes barefoot in winter because he had given his shoes and socks to a beggar. He once arrived coatless at Evensong, and not only coatless, having literally put his shirt on a vagrant. Heaven would, no doubt, regard such eccentricity as a normal albeit uncommon convention.

In 1950 two hill-farming brothers occupied the same house, but without ever speaking to each other. In their youth, I was told, they had fallen out over a girl, each suitor believing that she had rejected him on account of his brother. So for the next forty years the two bachelors remained mutually in Coventry. Their affairs were conducted via an intermediary who sat in the hall, exchanging scribbled messages which he passed to and fro between the kitchen and the parlour ("Your turn to mend that fence" and "You still owe me for last month's pig food").

People who cannot perceive their own eccentricity are as a rule to be pitied; but the deliberate and good-natured odd-man -out is as a rule to be admired because he either ignores or reduces interference by commerce, bureaucracy, and all other commissars. To those whom it may concern (if any such exist), I confess that I wear a Norfolk jacket, and dine by candlelight, and eat bread that does not taste like insipid chewing-gum. I speak of England when I mean England and of Westmorland when I mean Westmorland. In like manner I rate Robert Bridges incomparably higher than T. S. Eliot, and John Osborne abysmally lower than J. M. Synge. I stand up when I hear the National Anthem, and I move away when I hear a liar shouting; "Brothers, the truth is . . ." I do not believe that a leopard changes its spots overnight, nor that ethnic groups suddenly eradicate their congenital cruelty, idleness, bravery, discipline, or artistry. I regard politics as a necessary intrusion on the business of living, and I hold that sport should be a pastime of youngsters, not the obsession of an entire nation. I walk whenever it is not necessary to ride, and I regard motor-ways as I regard surgical operations—things to be avoided if that is reasonable and possible. I have several thousand books but no television set. I prefer cider to wine, and water to cider. I hope never to enter an aeroplane, and I intend never to join a trades union. I like people who can agree to differ, but I dislike people who describe motor-handbooks as "technical litrer-cher". I close the door brusquely on commercial travellers, but my home is open day and night to all good souls who are in distress, and to selected sinners likewise.

I assert, finally, that all men are born unequal; that most Britons take too much food and too little exercise; and that if fifty million of them could migrate to the Moon or some other place, this kingdom would then stand a sporting chance of becoming a green and pleasant land. So, as you see, my own part of the world contains at least one person who does not always conform with popular circles.

11

The Heroic Heath

"A Saturday afternoon in November was approaching the time of twilight, and the vast tract of unenclosed wild known as Egdon Heath embrowned itself moment by moment . . . The face of the heath by its mere complexion added half an hour to evening; it could in like manner retard the dawn, sadden noon, anticipate the frowning of storms scarcely generated, and intensify the opacity of a moonless night to a source of quaking and dread." So begins the first chapter of Thomas Hardy's *Return of the Native*, a famous piece of writing and a slap in the eye for those who share Keats's belief that all descriptions are bad. Both in prose and in poetry Hardy tended to creak, but his evocation of Egdon Heath rises to the summit of its theme, so that awe and foreboding ride rough-shod over any infelicities of style. One might say, indeed, that Egdon is the novel's hero because Hardy depicted it as far more impressive than Damon Wildeve or Clym Yeobright. Even the fiery Eustacia Vye felt intimidated by such lonely desolation.

Hardy himself admitted that Egdon is an amorphous region: "Under the general name of Egdon Heath, which has been given to the sombre scene of the story, are united or typified heaths of various names, to the number of at least a dozen; these being virtually one in character and aspect, though their original unity, or partial unity, is now somewhat disguised by intrusive strips and slices brought under the plough with varying degrees of success, or planted with woodland."

Despite encroachment of modern buildings, tracts of the heath exist as far eastward as Upton, a suburb of Bournemouth and Poole. Other tracts can be found on the road from Wimborne to Dorchester and also between the Rivers Frome and Puddle. Among the few heathland villages is Affpuddle, the place where Aeffa, a Saxon, held land near a *pedel* (marsh). In Hardy's novel the village appears as East Egdon, the scene of Clym's marriage to Eustacia.

Hardy put Dorset on the literary map as securely as Wordsworth put Lakeland, yet he never used the word *Dorset* in his fiction. Ultimately, of course, he ventured far beyond Dorset, thereby reviving the ancient name of Wessex. "The series of novels I projected," he explained, "being mainly of the kind called local, they seemed to require a territorial definition of some sort to lend unity. Finding that the area of a single county did not afford a canvas large enough for this purpose, and that there were no objections to an invented name, I disinterred the old one." Early editions of *The Return of the Native* contained a map which Hardy himself had drawn. In a letter to the publishers, Smith and Elder, he wrote: "I enclose a sketch-map of the supposed scene in which *The Return of the Native* is laid, copied from the one I used in writing the story; and my suggestion is that we place an engraving of it as frontispiece in the first volume . . . I am of opinion that it would be a desirable novelty." Wessex was the kingdom of the Gewissas or 'West Saxons', whose most famous rulers were Ine and Alfred. Some people are surprised that Hardy should have included Oxford and Aldershot in Wessex, which they regard as part of the west country. However, the kingdom did at one time extend as far as Sussex and the Upper Thames.

Although Hardy invented most of his place-names (Sandbourne for Bournemouth, Christminster for Oxford), it is possible to identify several of the Egdon sites. Thus, Damon Wildeve kept an inn (Hardy called it 'The Quiet Woman') whose original name, 'The Traveller's Rest', was changed to 'The Duck', whereafter the public house became a private one. Bloom's End, the home of the Yeobrights, may have been a cottage near Heedless William's Pond, not a great distance from Hardy's birthplace at Higher Bockhampton, where he wrote *Under the Greenwood Tree* and *Far from the Madding*

Crowd. Some of the characters in *The Return of the Native* bear names that blend fact with fantasy. Eustacia, for example, was named after the wife of a fifteenth-century lord of the manor at Ower Moigne, which appears in the novel as Nether Mynton. Eustacia's husband, Clym, was named after Clement le Hardy, a Jerseyman whom Hardy claimed as an ancestor, and whose lordly '*le*' he wished to adopt, but was dissuaded therefrom.

From a knoll near his birthplace Hardy could see Egdon Heath: "A Face", he called it, "on which Time makes but little impression". Not even a bright May morning can wholly dispel Egdon's sombre somnolence. The paucity of hedges and trees reduces the number and species of birds that might have enlivened the silence; and in high summer a hot day finds the walker vainly seeking shelter from the sun. At night, if an owl does screech, the sound can be heard a mile away. Hardy's opening chapter shows Egdon as a nether region, poised between autumn and winter, between afternoon and night. To explore it at that hour and at that season is to share something of Hardy's projection of his own pessimism onto an object which is neither gloomy nor glad. Seen against November twilight, each hillock looms like a bald brown head, and in the hollows a stunted tree winces at the wind. You can walk a long way without passing a house. If you are very far-sighted, or extremely imaginative, you may persuade yourself that you have glimpsed the sea which fascinated Eustacia Vye's father, of whom Hardy remarked: "He had been, in his day, a naval officer . . ."

In some places, then, the heath remains uncultivated and scarcely worth reclaiming. In other places it is a training ground for Army tanks. Elsewhere a few cattle and sheep nibble the grass, or get whatever they can from the bracken and gorse which in Hardy's youth gave employment to furze-cutters. Wandering across Egdon Heath on a November evening, you understand why Hardy said: "It had a lonely face suggesting tragical possibilities." Nevertheless, there are moments when a reader wishes that Hardy had created just one leading character who lived a long and predominantly happy life.

In a Monastery Garden

On Remembrance Sunday a few years ago I was in Eire, exploring a countryside as deep as any in these islands. Noticing a green mound, I asked a farmer about it.

"Did you not know?" he replied, evidently dismayed by my ignorance. "A monastery stood there."

"Oh," I exclaimed, feeling ashamed because I had often chided tourists who, although they take wine at dinner, will not pay the price of a guidebook. "Tell me about it," I said.

"In the blessed past," the farmer explained, "when men spelt 'God' with a capital G and actually believed in Him, they built a monastery on this spot. A very holy place it was. And the monks were holy, too—so holy they'd not lift a finger to defend themselves, though they'd no objection at all if someone offered to defend 'em gratis and for nothing. In short, they were a pack o' pacifists, the like will stand by while their own folk are being slaughtered." Here the farmer crossed himself and then spat piously. "I'm thinking even a lamb makes a fight for its life."

"But . . ."

"But there was one monk with guts in his entrails. Brother Barnabas they called him. A great roaring ranting fella he was, the like you seldom see nowadays, outside o' the lunatic Left. But whereas the Left is a Niagara of nonsense, Brother Barnabas was that wise he'd have made Solomon himself sound like a dunce in the corner." Here the farmer broke off to ask: "Have you any history at all?"

"A little," I hoped.

"Then you'll know already, there was a great plague o'pirates in these parts, fellas with an eye to the main chance, especially if she was pretty. Anyway, Brother Barnabas warned the monks that the pirates was on the war path. 'Arm yourselves,' he said. But he might just as well have told Satan to sign the pledge. Well, sure enough the pirates came. They burned the monastery, they raped the women, they stole the sheep. Among the seven surviving monks was Brother

Barnabas. He'd the sense to hide himself, away in what we call Finnigan's Wood."

"Did the survivors . . .?"

"They did indeed, led by Barnabas. They rebuilt the whole place. But the minute they'd finished, back came the pirates. This time there was only five monks left, so Brother Barnabas said, 'Bloody Hell . . .' "

"Barnabas did?"

"Sure, I was speaking metabolically. The point is, he refused to do any more rebuilding unless the other four agreed to dig a ditch and learn the art o' self-defence. Mind you, he'd a terrible time to start with. Three of 'em couldn't tell a bow from an arrow. But in the end he taught 'em, and when reinforcements arrived he soon had a well-trained Home Guard. What's more he'd a flame-thrower."

"Indeed?"

"Deeds is louder than words when you're parleying with pirates. Of course, he'd another terrible tussle trying to persuade the monks to use the weapon. 'Oh,' they said, 'it's a heathen device.' 'Heathen?' he shouted. 'Who the Hell else do you suppose we're up against?' " Once more the farmer spat. "Well, back came the boys, thinking they was on to another good thing. But ten minutes later not one of 'em was left alive. Sprawled in the ditch they was, dead as yesterday's racing results."

"And the monks?"

"Not a scratch. The ditch and the flames had saved 'em. Only the cat got killed, and only because it came home late, which was its own fault and probably another cat's also. And did the news spread! Never a pirate from here to Penzance hadn't heard o' Brother Barnabas and his battling brethren. For twenty years there was peace in the land, and the monks prayed, and the people prospered, and the rain came more or less when it wasn't wanted."

"It all sounds . . ."

"Too good to be true? You're right and twice over, for the monks grew old and then too old, and the young ones was after being pacifists again. So the ditch decayed, the flame-thrower rotted, and the brothers took to using their arrows to stake the sweet peas. Barnabas warned 'em, mind, but they'd not listen.

So the news got around again, and so did the pirates. In ten minutes they'd over-run the place and was pawning the candlesticks."

"What," I asked, "about Brother Barnabas?"

The farmer pointed toward Finnigan's Wood. "But when he emerged he was that mad he out-cussed Jehovah and Yaweh and all the rest o' the biblical blasphemers. Sure, there's nothing in the Scriptures to touch him for holy imprecation. 'I'm through with you,' he said. 'You're all a pack o' euphonious eunuchs chanting psalms in a smouldering ruin.' And Barnabas went away, so he did, and lived to a great age . . . though you've not to believe 'em when they tell you he was 106 at the time of his second marriage. A Protestant invented the story and got it wrong. Brother Barnabas never married. Never married at all. Neither once nor twice. And he was only eighty-eight when he took a doxy to cherish his declining aftermath."

"A remarkable story," I observed.

"It's not at all remarkable," the farmer replied. "It's being repeated throughout the world. Your own nation told the story in 1914 and again in 1939, and they still are telling it . . . with the Russians sitting rapt as an audience who've got in without paying. But one thing's for sure. There's a monastery not ten thousand miles from where we are now, and there the brethren did defend themselves, and the monastery's still standing, having done good deeds for a thousand years. But this place . . ." he glanced at the lonely mound, "this is a Golgotha, a place of numbskulls who'd watch an innocent man being murdered but wouldn't stop the murder by killing the murderer."

Striding into Winter

Mid-morning coffee in the garden, with the sun so bright that you blink: June is it, or July, or September's final fling? None of them; it is November, a month commonly equated with Housman's bleak prospect:

> Around the thudding homesteads
> The leafless timbers roar . . .

Having sipped your coffee, you litanize the flowers that bloom in the autumn—asters, dahlias, pansies, petunias, roses, marigolds, forget-me-nots, and one lupin gallantly and freakishly recovering from its partial decapitation by an August gale. The air is so calm that a falling leaf has time to perform a graceful ballet before reaching the ground. Such, then, is the scene which November may unfold as an interlude between the autumnal gales and the wintry frosts.

Fiona Macleod knew that the autumnal tints are best seen against a cloudless sky: "The most subtle charm of the November woods," she wrote, "is in those blue spaces which lie at so brief a distance in every avenue of meeting boughs, under every enclosing branch." What the leaves lack in numbers they supply in colours. The cherry and the wild service vie for first prize, each as vivid as a pink-coated huntsman; but the holly's staid foliage will flourish when the rest have fallen. The effects of light and shade are dramatic, the frontier being marked as precisely as the coloured contours on a map, so that the shadow cast by a barn turns the grass black, yet beyond the blackness the grass shines like a cricket pitch after rain. Grazing alone in a paddock, the pony still needs to swish his tail against the insects. Birds, by contrast, show no sign of life until a robin sings, and even he sounds tame, as though aware that no rival will retrieve the gauntlet of his song.

Clear visibility and the thinning hedgerows reveal objects which have been hidden since April. Householders who boasted: "There's no other building in sight" now find themselves quizzed by distant farms; and having walked to the top of the hill, they discover that their house is not at all an eyrie but can be plainly seen behind its pallisade of leafless oaks. Indoors, the rooms are flooded with light. Midges circumnavigate a sunbeam while wasps carve noughts-and-crosses on the window's transparent barrier. Motes of dust on chair-covers gleam like miniscule amber, and the ashes in the hearth suggest that within three hours the temperature may reach shivering point. For how much longer will these halcyon moments last? Taking no chances, you make several sorts of hay while the sun does shine, beginning with a walk through the wood, where you marvel once again at the never-failing novelty of the all-familiar tints.

Last month's green path through the glade is paved now with a copper-coloured carpet on which the yellow oaks and the lemon sycamores have stitched their own haphazard patterns. Since the path stands a foot above the surrounding soil, you can navigate the dark nights by sound alone, knowing that you have strayed from the path whenever your footsteps rustle the leaves in the hollow beside it. A gap in the trees reveals a cottage whose owner is trundling a wheelbarrow to a waste patch beyond his wood shed, whence a pleasingly pungent pyre confirms that Laurence Binyon's season has arrived:

> Now is the time for the burning of the leaves.
> They go up in fire: the nostril pricks with smoke . . .

Glancing round, you are surprised by the speed at which the daylight is failing; but having emerged from the wood, you discover that the apparent failure was caused by a bank of clouds approaching from the north-west. Like a domed lid, the invaders close over the sky until only a small segment of blue remains; then that, too, darkens, and the temperature drops while the wind rises. You turn for home, hoping to arrive before the rain. While you walk, the leaves sigh, stir and finally take off like frightened birds, some to be impaled on the tree from which they fell, some to slap themselves against a wall, some to fly out of sight. The carpet, however, remains intact, being woven of innumerable autumns that lie a series of buried sylvan civilizations.

November was the Roman *novem*, or ninth month of the year. Today, as the penultimate month, it continues to follow the devices and desires of its own heart, alternately blustering, freezing, raining, snowing, and—on or about St Martin's Day—granting a glimpse of summer. But all such glances are brief. Very soon the wind and the frost will strip the last of the leaves in a demolition that steals the picture by opening up distant prospects while at the same time drawing attention to the leaves themselves, either as frail relics on a tree or as sections of a carpet on the ground. The largest accumulation of leaves will be found among the hollows in a beechwood. I have known Chiltern woods that were paved four feet deep. If you jumped into them, the leaves flew above your head. If you walked through them, they pirouetted round your knees. Some, from the lowermost layer, were scarcely more than mould. Others were limp with the rainfall of preceding weeks. Not even the strongest gale could erode the tightly-packed debris. As each layer disintegrated, so a younger one took its place.

During the winter of his own long life, Robert Bridges walked through a November wood, trampling the leaves:

> And all their ravisht beauty
> Strewn 'neath my feet today
> Rustles as I go striding
> Upon my wintry way.

High Life

Is life on a hill more agreeable than life in a valley? That question is being raised by the gale which now batters this house, whereof the walls, although they are two feet thick, shudder whenever a gust smites them. The wind booms down the chimney, whistles past the window, whines under the door, and generally maintains an incessant din, like aircraft circling overhead. Such is the price of living in a house that tallies somewhat with Edward Thomas's description of Gordon Bottomley's north country cottage:

> It stands alone
> Up in a land of stone . . .
> A land of rocks and trees
> Nourished on wind and stone.

The men who built my house three centuries ago did their best to shield it from the elements by setting it just below the brow of a hill which takes the sting from an easterly wind. Against a south-wester they or their successors planted a small wood which certainly breaks the force of a gale but so amplifies the sound that an apparent take-off by the entire roof is found to be merely the wind thundering through the trees. A later generation planted a row of beeches along the drive; and they, too, served as a windbreak, but they also obscured a splendid vista, so I felled them and accepted the consequences. At present, therefore, I can almost see the wind, goading the trees as it did on Wenlock Edge:

> The gale, it plies the saplings double,
> And thick on Severn snow the leaves.

But I do not complain, because a house on a hill enjoys several advantages over a house in a valley. For example, the chrysanthemums in my garden thrive while those in the combe are blackened by frost. No matter how profusely the heavens may open, their cargo cannot drown this house, for the spate surges downhill, gathering flotsam *en route*. Though I may one day see my tiles flying from the roof, I shall never watch my furniture floating on the floor. These foul-weather compensations ought really to be rated as all-weather advantages, not least because a lowlander must crick his neck in order to scan summits which a highlander confronts on equal terms. Moreover, the confrontation may take place through a window, thereby enabling the spectator to become an armchair traveller when the weather, or some other impediment, deters him from making a more active journey.

Since my house stands almost eight hundred feet above the sea, it is by British standards high and by southern English standards very high, though far short of the highest. If we ask: "Where *is* Britain's highest house?" we shall receive contradictory answers; but if we ask: "Where *was* Britain's highest house?" we shall find ourselves on firm and lofty ground because the house crowned Ben Nevis, more than four thousand feet among the clouds. It was, in fact, part of an observatory from which scientists observed the weather and other natural phenomena. Life at that altitude was exhilarating, especially in 1898, when a thermometer, hanging only six feet from the kitchen stove, registered two degrees of frost, and the wind exceeded 150 miles an hour. After a few decades of useful work the observatory was closed through lack of money.

At Alston in Cumberland I once met a man who claimed that his own house was the highest in England. When pressed to justify the claim, he replied that the house overlooked Alston, and that Alston itself was England's highest market town (a precedence disputed by Buxton in Derbyshire). But

private houses are not the only contestants in this matter; witness 'The Cat and Fiddle' in Cheshire and the Tan Hill Inn in Yorkshire, both of which have claimed to be England's highest tavern (the latter wins by a few feet). A comparable rivalry used to exist between Braemar and Tomintoul, each claiming to be the highest village in the Scottish Highlands (the latter wins by ten yards). There is no doubt at all about the identity of England's highest railway station: it stands at Dent Head in Yorkshire, on the old Midland Railway from London to Scotland.

Meantime, the gale still rages, gathering strength as the light fails. If I open the front door, a torrent of twigs rushes in. If I open a window, the curtains become parachutes. The garden is a litter of straw, pebbles, fleece, and one gumboot in search of its mate. Twice the hurricane lamp has been bowled over, and now it sways like a drunken moon on a rusty nail. Segments of tin roof from a distant cattle-shed are mimicking the needle that stuck in the groove of a very long-playing contemporary quartet. The drive to the house looks as though a giant has passed by, snapping branches as a child plucks flowers. The fish pond is a miniature ocean, surging whitely against concrete cliffs. Like submarines, the fish lie low. Now the electricity has failed, leaving me to meditate on Man's conquest of Nature. I can only trust in Housman's weather forecast:

> The gale, it plies the saplings double,
> It blows so hard, 'twill soon be gone . . .

All in all, then, it is what the sailors call a thick night. Yet I still prefer to live high up rather than low down. For one thing, I am nearer the sun; for another, the air is more bracing; for a third, I rather like to sit in fireside candle-glow while the wind howls, and the rain hisses, and the house in the valley watches the river rise and shine all over the kitchen floor.

12

On the Road to Heaven

On a lonely part of the moor, far from any village, stands a small and solitary building which at first sight seems to serve the Electricity Board. "What a pity," you exclaim, "to put such an eyesore in such beautiful surroundings." But the men who did put it there believed otherwise, for the architecture pleased them, and the site was chosen after a careful survey of the scattered cottages and farms. In short, the building is a Nonconformist chapel.

I happened to pass that chapel, late in the afternoon, during choir practice. Three cars stood outside, flanked by four bicycles, one of them a woman's. A sheepdog was tethered to the iron railings. Suddenly the lights were switched on, followed by some tentative notes from a harmonium. Then, through the dusk, I heard a familiar invitation: "O come, all ye faithful, joyful and triumphant . . ."

Protestant Nonconformity always has been strait-laced and inclined to spiritual pride. "Art thou saved?" is often a way of stating: "I *am* saved, thanks to the Latterday Brotherhood." Why, one asks, did the British countryside produce such a crop of chapels? It cannot have been solely for doctrinal reasons. After all, few villagers could give an accurate account of the *Logos* according to Luther or Zwingli or Melancthon. As for John Wesley, he is still depicted as a Radical Dissenter, though he lived and died as a High Tory and an Anglican priest who at Epworth and Wroot had celebrated Mass, heard confession and abstained from wine during Lent. Wesley's mission was to revive, not to undermine, the English Church. So we are left to ask again, why does Britain contain such a crop of chapels? The simplest answer is also the least unsatisfactory: chapels enabled the cottagers to snub the Church in general and the squire in particular.

Religious dissent, then, marched hand-in-hand with political dissent, each finding most of its supporters among those admirable private enterprisers whom Marx detested, the farm labourers, the small shopkeepers, the self-employed artisans. Ultimately, of course, the Anti-Establishers founded their own Establishment, which became far less tolerant than the Anglican. There is a paradox in all this, because Luther and Calvin abhorred political democracy. Calvin, indeed, imposed on Geneva a theocracy which not even Hildebrand would have dared to create. In 1537 he ordered his henchmen to pursue and if necessary to exterminate all who dissented from dissent. "Let the pastors," he wrote, "slay the wolves." And when Calvin wrote "slay" he meant it. Hussites and Quakers were not the only subject of *De Heretico Comburendo*. Nevertheless without the English Dissenters, this kingdom during the nineteenth century might have suffered civil war. As it was, the chapelfolk leavened their political demands with patriotic moderation. Most of the early trades unionists were themselves Dissenters, willing to render unto Caesar but not willing to accept starvation wages. Two centuries after Cromwell's Roundheads had been disbanded, Richard Jefferies described the Wiltshire Dissenters as "men who reproduced in themselves the character of those close-cropped soldiers". At the same time, he emphasized that the best of them were "conspicuous for upright steadiness, and irreproachable moral conduct, with some surly independence". William Morris, on the other hand, exhibited the arrogance of a Socialist intellectual when he sneered at "the Wesleyan-unsympathetic-with-Art". But Morris is dead, and the Dissenters are not. Mellowed by experience, and no longer throttled with a temperance ribbon, they remain as bastions of Leftish politics, hortatory eloquence, altruistic self-help, and a firm conviction that (in Voltaire's words) "An Englishman goes to Heaven by the road which pleases him."

As theologians, the rural Dissenters were noted for Fundamentalism and a preoccupation with Hell fire. Commenting on Calvinism, Maurice Lindsay declared: "It has deprived more Scots people of the power of passionately savouring life than any other single force, simply by inculcating the belief that the absolute enjoyment of life militates against the enjoyment of the after-life which Christian teachings promised." As corporate worshippers, however, the Dissenters displayed a zeal and brotherliness which too often shamed, or ought to have shamed, the vicarage. As politicians, they launched a bloodless revolution whose legacy includes the closed shop, the suicidal strike and the erosion of Christian teaching in State schools. The old Wesleyan Liberals would have regarded modern Britain as a nation of godless and gutless wastrels, governed not by the government but by the shop stewards who coerce the government.

There is, of course, a wide gulf between the various Dissenters. On the one hand are the Unitarians, who for many years represented the intellectual élite; on the other hand are the diehard Scots, some of whom still forbid their bairns to pull a cracker on Christmas Day. Like every other Christian group, the Dissenters are grievously depleted. Some sects have disappeared, others have merged, a few continue to fight the good fight in glorious isolation and under such names as Primitive Adventists and Reformed Reformationists. Although certain aspects of the Nonconformist temperament are vulnerable to mockery, truth achieves a more charitable perspective by observing whatever is best in the hearts of a chapel congregation while they strive to reach Heaven by their own road.

Just such a chapel stands in an unfrequented combe about a mile from where I live. It is a plain yet comely building. In recent years the shepherdless congregation has sometimes consisted of only three people—a father, a mother and their daughter. Fine weather or foul, the trio walked down the steep hill and along the narrow track to their place of worship. The father read the Bible, the daughter played the harmonium, the mother took the collection. Not long ago the father died, and the chapel was put up for sale. Even an atheist may say of those three Dissenters: "Well done, ye good and faithful servants."

Winterscape

December is a dark month, and its gloomiest moments occur just before Christmas, when the shortest day reminds us that we may yet suffer the coldest weather. Coldness can, of course, be measured, whereas darkness is a vague quality, unless we take it to mean utter blackness, or simply the hours when motorists must use their headlights.

In Britain, of course, the weather is so changeable that even the murkiest winter day may go down in a blaze of glory. Peering through the window, soon after four o'clock in the afternoon, you notice that the light is ebbing from the fields and that a windless air suggests frost, though the grey sky predicts rain rather than ice. Either way, the outlook is dispiriting except insofar as it heightens the prospect of buttered toast by a beech-log fire. When you peer again, a quarter of an hour later, the half-light has become twilight. Venturing a few yards down the lane, you observe your own breath, wreathing like a dragon's.

Proceeding from the lane into a steep meadow, you observe that on one side of the combe, which has remained frosty all day, the grass gleams as if it had been sprinkled with sugar. You hear—or imagine that you hear—each brittle blade being tugged by the cow's tongue. Manure looks like coffee-coloured concrete. Frost has burned the bracken from dark brown to near-black. Flints in the furrows wink like little light-houses. After you have been walking for about five minutes, you catch sight of the first star. Perhaps you view it through eyes as wide as those of the two Lavenham ladies who confessed:

> Twinkle, twinkle, little star;
> How I wonder what you are . . .

Now the path bears north, climbing a skyline whose colour fades from dark blue to pale—palest of all where the hill carves an ebony arc. You unlatch a gate and enter a lane leading east. This lane is lined with trees which, in the deepening dusk, seem to form part of the sky itself. Some of them resemble candelabra that were designed to carry an uncountable number of candles; others might be brooms, or trellises, or a cluster of close-reefed masts. When the lane changes direction, the effect is dramatic because the trees create not so much an avenue as a tunnel whose far end reveals Wordsworth's "light of setting sun", with the scarlet flames turning yellow while they leap. Soon another gate appears, leading to an even steeper combe, crowned on the opposite side by conifers just visible where they reach the fiery sector; but the rest of the combe is so dark that you cannot tell where the brow falls away nor where the slope starts to climb again. Only the summit is seen, sombre and somnolent against the stars.

Approaching a cottage garden, you smell a bonfire whose smoke twines ropelike on the calm air. Having reached the cottage, you see that the bonfire is dormant; only the blue-grey plume signifies life. But when a breeze sidles through the combe, it penetrates the sodden leaves, causing a spark to leap up and become a flame; and soon the moribund mass is hissing, spitting, crackling. Hearing it, the cottager peers round the door, decides that all is well and returns to whatever he was doing. Half a minute later the breeze dies away and with it the flames.

All birds have gone to roost, and all are silent except the rooks, which maintain a strident lullaby. Sometimes the noise grows so shrill that you wonder whether it really is a lullaby (it sounds more like a tribal feud, or at least a broken marriage). Presently an airy rustle reveals six rooks returning belatedly to their latticed roost, where they swell the hubbub. When the din has ceased to occupy your thoughts, you become conscious of the cold. Turning from the gate, you find that the sunset has at last burned itself out, all save a few streaks which are neither red nor yellow but a duck's egg green. While you walk, the green streaks fade to a colour unrecorded in dictionaries, not grey, not blue, not black, but everywhere frosty and pricked with stars that create a constellated choreography wherein the dancers seem to move without motion. Day, in short, has died. Even its ghost has departed.

After nightfall, sound supplants colour as a calendar and clock. Foxes bark, invisible among bracken near a stream in the combe. During August the stream is inaudible until you stand beside it, but in December the spate echoes across the fields.

When the final rook has uttered its farewell caw, an owl chimes in, and a fieldmouse crosses the lane, not scurrying as at noon but leisurely, like a man who obeys the traffic lights. On reaching the other side of the lane, the mouse burrows into a bank and so records the temperature by crinkling the frozen leaves. From somewhere on the hills a sheep bleats twice. Perhaps a passing footstep causes the farm dog to growl. The rest is silence.

On high ground in deep country, where cars are few and not given to late journeys, you may test your knowledge of the terrain by plotting the course of the headlights on the farthest hill. "Now," you say, "he's just reached Mill Farm." Sure enough, the lights disappear as the car delves down to the stream. Visible once more, the lights turn left ("Past the crossroads now"), then right ("That'll be Tor Copse"), and then due west ("He's making for Three Barrows"). It is unlikely that you will meet anyone in the lane, but if you do, the traveller will almost certainly be someone you recognize, and the ancient greetings are exchanged: "Another frost tonight" . . . "Dry, though and that's something to be thankful for after all that rain."

Home again, on the garden path, you avoid a puddle. Less than an hour ago that puddle was water; now it is ice. From the porch, you take a last look at the last segment of the last month of what will soon become the last year:

> Now dims the sky, now dance the stars,
> Now shine the silver-slanting bars
> Of moonlight on the ice
> Tightening a silent vice.

A Modern Christmas Card

In a village shop the other afternoon I noticed among the Christmas cards a reproduction of a Victorian painting of a farmhouse kitchen, showing a family seated before an open hearth where a sooty kettle hung from a blackened chain, and a collie slept alongside a cat in a sewing-basket. Tied to the rafters, four succulent hams were taking a leisurely cure. Part of the kitchen table had been laid for a meal; the remaining space carried a book and a pair of spectacles. A shepherd's crook leaned against the grandfather clock. At first sight the log fire seemed too red to be real, and the family sitting round it seemed likewise to be not of this world, so pink were their cheeks, so conspicuous their domestic concord. A cynic would have dismissed the scene as sentimental.

Returning from the village, which lay in a region far from my home, I was surprised when a woman at a farm-gate pointed her finger in the direction from which I had walked. I glanced back, wondering whether I was about to be impaled by a runaway bull. But no such thing; the lane was empty. Then the woman shouted: "It's yours!" Again I glanced back, and this time I saw a wake of white sugar.

"The bag has burst," the woman called, adding: "They'll be shut by now." After that she invited me to step indoors while she fetched some sugar from her own larder.

Down a stone-flagged passage we went and thence into a scene which a cynic would yet again have dismissed as sentimental. There blazed the logs, as red as in the painting. There sat the family, no less pink-cheeked and cordial. Yet the artist had been right to pile on his colours, because he, too, saw the kitchen against a background of twilight filtering through uncurtained windows. A collie basked beside the fire, while a cat made both ends meet in a cardboard box. Part of the table had been laid for a meal; the remaining space carried a jig-saw puzzle, a farming magazine, and a pair of spectacles. Needless to say, neither the room nor its occupants were replicas of those in the painting. True, a chain still hung from the chimney, but it had been polished to serve as an ornament, like the two brass candlesticks. A gleaming electric kettle replaced the sooty one, and the yard outside was no longer fouled by a herd nor polluted by a privy. However, several hens strutted there, and a shepherd's crook hung from a nail on the barn door. Moreover, the kitchen's inner life remained basically the same, insofar as the three generations really did love one another and therefore really did forgive (or very nearly forgive) those quirks and peccadillos which form a large part of human nature. In some other homes, no doubt, the adolescents were muttering: "For God's sake, let's get out of here. The pub will open soon." In some other homes the children were frustrated, or bullied, or spoiled. But this roost was ruled by an amity whose symbols were kindly manners and a warm welcome. No one who lives in deep country will be surprised by the words that greeted me, a stranger: " 'Tis frosty weather. Happen thee'd like a cup o' summat. I know grandad would. T'owd fella's always ready for tay." Then, to the toddling grandchild: "Charley, lad, gie ower a beet an' let the gentleman warm hisself."

From time immemorial the kitchen has been the hub of a farmhouse. In 1590 the word 'kitchen' served as a verb, meaning 'to entertain in the kitchen'. In 1616 the English were still repeating an old maxim: "The first foundation of a good home must be the kitchen." Parlours did exist, but they were museums, open only on Sunday or for weddings and funerals. When Carl Moritz, a German pastor, toured England in 1782, he described a kitchen at Nettlebed in Oxfordshire: "The room served as a combined living and eating room. All round its walls were shelves for pewter dishes and plates, while from the ceiling hung an abundance of provisions such as loaves of sugar, sausages, sides of bacon, and so on."

William Howitt knew the eighteenth-century farmhouses when labourers lodged there as members of the family. "At night," he wrote, "a farmer takes his ease on the settle, under the old wide chimney—his wife and her worktable set near—the wenches darning their socks or making a cap for Sunday, and the men sitting on either side of the hearth, with their shoes off." During the nineteenth century, however, William Cobbett complained that many farmers were affecting gentility in a house "crammed with sofas, pianos and all sorts of fooleries". The kitchen, he added, had become "too neat for a dirty-shod carter to be allowed to come into it". When Richard Jefferies set the late Victorian scene, the farmhouse parlour had ceased to be a museum and was competing with the kitchen as a background for social occasions. Yet the old ways died hard, for Jefferies reported that many a Wiltshire housewife "still bakes bread in the oven at home. She makes all sorts of preserves, and wines too—cowslip, elderberry, ginger . . ."

Three facts have restored something of the kitchen's ancient status as the hub of the home: first, the multiplicity of domestic gadgets; second, the dearth of domestic servants; third, the cost of domestic fuel. Few folk can afford to employ a resident maid and to keep several rooms permanently heated. Families whose parents were served in the dining-room now serve themselves in the kitchen, and, instead of withdrawing to another room, they stay where they are, having washed their own dishes. When, therefore, the farmer and his men return home after a day's work, their kitchens are still recognizable as the hub which greeted John Clare's Christmas Eve:

> As the warm blaze cracks and gleams
> The supper reeks in savoury steams
> Or kettle simmers merrily
> And tinkling cups are set for tea.

In the Van of Progress

Gumbooted and macintoshed against the rain this morning, seven people huddle beside a wall near the church. Four of them are women; the fifth is a retired farmer, the sixth is an off-duty postman, the seventh is a small boy, and all live either in or near a hamlet comprising three farms and a dozen cottages.

Had the group been better-dressed, a stranger might suppose that they are early arrivals for divine service; but their workaday clothes and their facial expressions—neither very solemn nor especially cheerful—suggest either that they have met by chance or that they are reluctant to leave the sheltering wall. Their conversation, however, offers a clue to their mission, as when one of the women states: "I didn't care for his latest. Too much sex." Then the retired farmer remarks: "Us'm away to Spain come Saturday. Hoping to see the sun for a change. So the wife said I'd to learn the Spanish for 'toilet' and 'cider'."

As the church clock strikes ten, the group glance uplane while the child wipes the raindrops from a scrap of paper in his left hand. The postman observes: "Harry's pretty punctual as a rule. The only time I've ever known him really late was when the telly showed a programme about violence on the telly. He told me afterwards there was a master rush for anything about violence. In fact, one chap in the queue punched him on the nose."

Two minutes later a large black van hoots its way round the sharp bend. The van is marked "Mobile Library", and into it the group hurry, as much for shelter as for literature. Several hundred books are ranged attractively on the shelves, chiefly fiction but with a generous ration of travelogues, biographies, hobbies, and practical manuals. Poetry is absent.

By their books shall ye know them. The spectacled spinster, for instance, chooses *Exmoor in Prehistory, Geology Today*, and *The Story of the Alps*. The merry widow, on the other hand, whose hair is præternaturally yellow, prefers *Byron's Women, Better Sight Without Glasses*, and *The Battered Blonde*. The retired farmer has taken *First Steps in Spanish* and *Hints for Home Brewers*. His third choice, *The Moors in Spain*, has been made because he assumes that Moors are moorlands. When the small boy presents the scrap of paper, the librarian shakes his head at each of the three requests, which are *Mediæval Life in Colour, Post-Freudian Trends*, and "any book about arthritis". Having drawn so many blanks, the child selects *Model Railways, Ten Famous Murders*, and *Vintage Cars*. The postman's choice is *Betting for Profit* and *The Nude in Florentine Art*.

Snippets of conversation reveal the hamlet's literary tastes. Thus, the shepherd's sister confesses: "I always read the last page first 'cause I can't a-bear not to know who's done it." The woman from a remote farm confesses: "My dear soul, I've no time for book-reading, not with a husband and five young children. But I do walk yere now and again, just to meet folks and keep up with the latest news. The TV tells what's happening in Tokyo, but it don't never seem to get as far as South Molton and West Buckland." This pursuit of knowledge is not always mutual, for one of the women complains: "Ever since my eldest read *In the Steps of Stalin*, her's been nagging us to go to Russia next year. 'Not a hope,' I said. 'Your Dad's already booked rooms at Clacton, and that's as far east as you'm likely to get. Anyhow,' I said, 'why bother to go all the way to Russia? Just hang around any factory nowadays and you'll hear 'em speaking pure Bolshie.'" Now and again a borrower apologizes for having failed to return a book on time.

"Us couldn't think where it 'ad got to. Searched high and low
we did. I even 'ad Cissie looking in the hairing cupboard. But
we found it in the end. Grandad 'ad used it to wedge the garage
door. No 'arm done, mind. In fact, it's ironed out some o' the
wrinkles. Funny, when you come to think of it, 'cause the book
was called *'Ome Tips for 'Ouseholders*. Ah, and it 'ad a chapter
specially about doors."

During a walk from London to John o' Groats in 1864, an
American farrier, Elihu Burritt, noticed that even the humblest
Scottish home contrived to buy good books: "You will," he
wrote, "seldom find a cottage in Scotland, however poor or
small, without a shelf of books in it." English farmhands were
far less enterprising; few of them ever read a book review.
Writing a century ago, Richard Jefferies reported that "The
villager is in utter ignorance of books in the publishers'
warehouses in London." Nevertheless, the book trade did have
a few self-employed commercial travellers, for Jefferies admitted that "Some little traffic in books, or pamphlets rather,
goes on now in rural places through the medium of pedlars."
Although Jefferies would have approved the Mobile Libraries,
his attitude differed from ours because he assumed that most
people would buy books, not borrow them. He himself lived at
a time when copies of many of the English classics were
published at a price equivalent to two new pence apiece, which
meant that all save the poorest households could buy twenty or
thirty books every year.

As an author, Jefferies might have said: "If thousands of
people read my books without paying me a farthing, how do
you expect me to live?" At the very least he would have said:
"If the people who do read my books were each to pay me one
penny per volume, I might then earn nearly as much as an
unskilled labourer." Either way, he would certainly have
added: "The writing of literature is not a hobby, indulged after
a day's work at an office or a factory. Nor is the act of writing
the whole of writing. An artist must spend much time reading,
observing, thinking." In short, Jefferies believed that an
author may reasonably ask to be paid a small sum by everybody
who takes home a copy of his book. After all, we do not expect
to 'borrow' bread from a baker. On the contrary, if one loaf
could somehow meet the needs of a hundred families, only a

madman would enter the bakery business; and even he might take offence when his non-paying customers said: "You should consider yourself lucky to sell any bread at all. Besides, think how much pleasure the world gets from eating your free loaves."

Shap of the Fells

Some, we were told, are born great; some achieve greatness; and some have greatness thrust upon them. My dog has scored the hat-trick. He was born great, of an ancient family; he achieved greatness, being brave, gentle, faithful; and greatness was thrust upon him by most of the television studios in England. And there at once I pause, lest praise of a dog should lapse—or even seem to lapse—into praise of a dog's master. However, the two lives are so interwoven that they cannot be wholly separated, and I must therefore bask in my dog's reflected glory.

Some people dislike dogs; others cannot understand why dogs arouse deep affection in their owners; and everyone has blushed at the person who treats an animal as though it were a human being. All who do keep a dog know that their own animal is (with certain trivial reservations) a paragon of canine excellence. Ralph Hodgson certainly knew so when he praised the bull terrier which accompanied him wherever he went,

> And hailed me blest o'er all, who am
> Her bondsman and her bard.

I first learned of my dog's existence from a friend who judged Lakeland Terriers in Westmorland. Together, therefore, we visited a place near Shap Fell, where we found a puppy so small that he could stand in the palm of my hand, and so young that the breeders doubted whether he should leave his mother. In the end he did leave, travelling three hundred miles in a cardboard box lined with straw. For reasons which I have now forgotten, our homeward journey halted at Shipston-on-Stour in Warwickshire, where—attached to a yard of string— the puppy stopped the traffic, stole the show, and generally accustomed himself to the limelight by attempting to devour a brace of Alsatians. Not for nothing had his ancestors been bred as Hunt terriers, game enough to tackle a fox at bay. In due time the puppy was registered as Shap of the Fells.

When Shap was about a year old, his master received an invitation to make a series of television travelogues. Halfway

through the first filming the producer—a young woman— decided that the dog was better-looking than his master, and ought therefore to be seen alongside him. From then onward the dog became a public figure. His photograph appeared in magazines and newspapers. He received (and declined) a request to advertise dog food. A sizeable fan mail reached him, together with collars, biscuits, bones, and a plea to lend someone £5 with which to buy a spaniel. None of that adulation went to his head. Like the Westmorlanders themselves, he cared little for the bright lights. He preferred dawn over Barbon Fell, and noon on Plynlimmon, and moonlight at Kinder Scout.

Despite his saintly disposition, Shap was once arrested and locked in the cells. The incident occurred when he and I were engulfed and then separated by a large crowd at a Scottish festival. Having sought him in vain, I inquired at the local police station. "He's quite safe," the sergeant assured me. "We recognized him at once. We've often seen him on the telly. So we put him in the cells." Shap has travelled widely. He visited John o' Groats three times and Land's End four times. He climbed Ben Nevis, Helvellyn, Plynlimmon, Cross Fell, and Dunkery Beacon. He walked the Roman roads from Roxburghshire to Cornwall and from Cardiganshire to Suffolk. He walked the prehistoric roads, too, along the Icknield Way, the Berkshire Ridgeways and several green roads through Wales. In his prime he walked the Pennine Way from Derbyshire to Scotland, a stroll of 250 windswept miles. He has been patted by a Foreign Secretary, fed by a film star, groomed by an Admiral, chased by a bull. In his native Westmorland he won a first prize as the best Lakeland terrier in the district.

As befits a male from the mountains, he never was unduly demonstrative; but I truly believe that he would have laid down his life for his friend. Age seemed scarcely to touch him. In his twelfth year I could say what Edward Thomas said of his own elderly dog: "He was strong and hearty, and never had any wretchedness except when I threw a stick at him in anger. If I travelled twenty or thirty miles on the Downs, he would walk and run two or three times as far. There seemed no reason why he should not go on forever." In his thirteenth year Shap walked twenty miles between dawn and dusk and then asked for an after-dinner stroll. In his fourteenth year, however, his sight and hearing lost something of their keenness, and on cold mornings he kept to his basket. In his sixteenth year the back legs grew stiff, and I began to wonder when the end would come. But not long ago, nearing his seventeenth year, he could still plod a mile uphill. Indeed, I had sometimes to restrain his doggedness lest he should strain his heart.

Last night he complained of not feeling well, and a few hours later he died, swiftly and easily, with his head in my hands. Such is the price of love, which exacts nothing less than a part of ourselves, great or small, according as the occasion and our temperament decree. A dog is, of course, only a dog. His death is universal and not new. Two thousand years ago a Greek countryman suffered a similar bereavement, whereof the monument was discovered by archæologists. "If," said the inscription, "you pass this way, and happen to notice this stone, do not laugh, even although it is only a dog's grave. Tears fell for my sake, and the earth was heaped above me by a master's hand, who likewise carved these words."